THE SEEKER'S GUIDE TO

Saints

Other books in the Seeker Series include

Living the Beatitudes Today
Bill Dodds and Michael J. Dodds, O.P.

The Seeker's Guide to Being Catholic
Mitch Finley

The Seeker's Guide to Reading the Bible
Steve Mueller

The Seeker's Guide to 7 Life-Changing Virtues
Bill Dodds and Michael J. Dodds, O.P.

The Seeker's Guide to the Christian Story
Mitch Finley

Chicago

THE SEEKER'S GUIDE TO

Saints

LOYOLAPRESS.
CHICAGO

MITCH FINLEY

LOYOLAPRESS.

3441 N. ASHLAND AVENUE
CHICAGO, ILLINOIS 60657

The Seeker Series from Loyola Press provides trustworthy guides for your journey of faith. It is dedicated to the principle that asking questions is not only all right, but essential.

The Scripture quotations contained herein are from the New Revised Standard Version Bible: Catholic Edition copyright © 1993 and 1989 by the Division of Christian Education of the National Council of the Churches of Christ in the U.S.A. Used by permission. All rights reserved.

Cover and interior design by Lisa Buckley
Cover image: Scala/Art Resource, NY

Library of Congress Cataloging-in-Publication Data

Finley, Mitch.
    The seeker's guide to saints / Mitch Finley.
        p. cm. — (Seeker series)
    Includes bibliographical references and index.
    ISBN 0-8294-1350-2
    1. Christian saints—Cult. 2. Catholic Church—
Doctrines. 3. Christian saints—Biography.
I. Title. II. Seeker series (Chicago, Ill.)

BX2333 .F56 2000   99-089239
235'.2—dc21   CIP

Printed in the United States of America
00 01 02 03 04 / 10 9 8 7 6 5 4 3 2 1

Contents

Acknowledgments

Thanks to Loyola Press editor LaVonne Neff for inviting me to write this book.

Thanks to the Sisters of St. Benedict, Monastery of St. Gertrude, Cottonwood, Idaho, who, in the 1950s, taught at Sts. Peter and Paul School, Grangeville, Idaho, for introducing me to the saints.

Thanks to my favorite saints, St. Mary, the mother of Jesus, St. Joseph, St. Paul, St. John the Evangelist, St. Isidore the Farmer, St. Teresa of Ávila, St. Jude, St. Anthony of Padua, St. Maximilian Kolbe, St. Thérèse of Lisieux, and Blessed André Bessette, and my favorite oughta-be saints, G. K. Chesterton, Caryll Houselander, Frank Sheed and Maisie Ward, Thomas Merton, and Pope John XXIII.

A Word to the Seeker

Saints enjoy a perennial popularity, and Catholics are not alone in their affection for saints. People of various religious persuasions are intrigued by saints. Something about the saints—their intimacy with the Divine Mystery, their wisdom, their inclination to thumb their noses at the world, their abundant common sense, or, frequently, their good humor—leads many people to seek more information about them. Perhaps the saints can help us learn more about God and more about the meaning and purpose of life, of our own lives in particular.

The perception that the saints can be helpful to us here and now is right on the money, for if the saints were anything during their lifetimes, they were seekers, not saints. The saints are saints, in the official sense, only in retrospect. Indeed, most saints laughed uproariously or scoffed indignantly at any suggestion that they were saints. If, however, someone suggested that he or she was a seeker (or some equivalent term), a saint would gladly acknowledge that this was the truth.

During his or her lifetime, a saint's daily existence was characterized by seeking the truth, living according to the truth, and, in more than a few cases, being ready to die for the truth. In this radical sense, therefore, the saints were and are the best models for anyone who tries to be a seeker today. The example, teaching, and companionship of the saints remain valuable for seekers of any era and culture.

The Seeker Series presumes that the reader is an open-minded person—perhaps Catholic, perhaps not—with honest questions, a person looking for direction in his or her life who is, at the very least, receptive to the possibility that Catholicism may shed some light on the quest. Therefore, here are the basic questions to which this book offers a reply: Who are the saints, and why does Catholicism celebrate saints and make a place for them in its faith, liturgy, and culture?

Sometimes people misunderstand who the saints are and what they are about. This book's purpose is to set the record straight. I want to give the saints their due and offer a look at their lives that is informative, inspiring, even entertaining. In a very real sense, we may view a saint as an image of God. Yes, saints are mere human beings, limited and sinful like us all. But in their passionate, extraordinary, pull-out-all-the-stops devotion to Christ, in their own historical circumstances, and through their unique personalities, they reflect and mediate something of God's love we might not see otherwise. A saint shows us God in a special manner.

You, dear reader, should be able to pick up this book, kick back, relax, begin to read, and soon find yourself astonished and captivated by some of the most remarkable people the world has ever known. Fair warning, however: Allow the saints to get close to your heart, and your life may change in ways you never could have predicted.

The purpose of *The Seeker's Guide to Saints* is to inspire us ordinary, struggling seekers to not give up hope and to keep on with our attempt to be faithful to the pilgrimage in our own time and place. This may not seem like much, but the saints would remind us that, in fact, it is everything.

The saints lived as seekers in their own cultures, at particular moments in history, with the resources they had at their disposal. When we read about them today we cannot simply take their words or their example at face value. Sometimes saints' actions will perplex us, or their words won't make sense. We need to "translate" from their historical and cultural situations to our own, so we will do that as we go along.

With that in mind, then, let us begin.

CHAPTER ONE

Who Are the Saints?

For Catholics, saints are not just heroes to admire from a distance. Saints are not like Charles Lindbergh, who in 1927 became a hero by flying nonstop across the Atlantic Ocean from New York to Paris for the first time ever. Saints are not even like humanitarian Clara Barton, who became a heroine to many by founding the American Red Cross on the battlefields of the Civil War. Rather, saints are Catholics who not only exhibited heroic holiness during their lifetimes but also are eternally alive fellow members of a community that transcends time and space.

The Communion of Saints

The traditional term for this transcendent community is *the communion of saints.* The *Catechism of the Catholic Church*

(992) points out that the term *communion of saints* appears in one of the oldest formulations of Christian faith, the Apostles' Creed, which concludes with these words: "I believe in the Holy Spirit, the holy catholic church, *the communion of saints,* the forgiveness of sins, the resurrection of the body, and life everlasting" (emphasis added).

Sometimes people study the saints or their writings to gather their wisdom, but they ignore or discount the fact that *the saints became saints precisely by living their Christian faith and by being the best Catholics they could be.*[1] They participated wholeheartedly in the sacramental life of the Catholic Church, and they had a deep respect for Catholic doctrines, official church teachings, and church leaders—even when, on occasion, they felt called to criticize those same leaders.

Of course, one may learn much from the saints by observing them "from the outside," as it were. But in order to truly understand the saints and the depth of their lives, one must take seriously the saints' Catholicism. For it was by being faithful to the deepest dimensions of their Catholic faith that saints and mystics ultimately transcended institutional and doctrinal boundaries to become universal men and women. They transcended those boundaries, but they never left them behind. To fail to grasp this truth is to fail to grasp the full meaning of the saints' lives and, in some cases, their writings.

In its broadest sense, *the communion of saints* refers to all of God's people, in this world and in the next, in time and in eternity. We belong to this community now, and we will continue to belong to it "on the other side." The same is true of all those who have gone before us, our loved ones and the countless souls we never knew in this world. Included too, of course, are "the saints" in the narrower sense, the relatively few people officially recognized by the Roman Catholic Church as being spiritual champions, if you will. This special group of saints is the subject of this book.

Prayer and Veneration

Because we belong to the same transcendent community the saints belong to, they can be our friends and companions as we make our pilgrimage through time and space. Just as we pray for one another here on earth, we may ask the saints to pray for us in heaven. It is only in this sense that we "pray to" the saints. We ask for their intercession, that is, their prayers to God on our behalf, but the saints have no power independent of God's power.

One of the most widely misunderstood aspects of Catholicism is its *veneration* of saints. Not only do people of other religious and philosophical persuasions sometimes harbor mistaken notions about the role of saints in Catholicism, but Catholics themselves sometimes have unbalanced ideas about saints.

To say that Catholics venerate saints simply means that we honor them and ask them to pray for us. Nothing more,

WHO ARE THE SAINTS?

and nothing less. This custom goes back to the early days of the Christian community. We know that as early as the mid–second century, Christians, in their liturgies, called upon those who had died as martyrs for the faith, asking for their prayers.[2] "Indeed, St. Lawrence, St. Cyprian of Carthage, and Pope St. Sixtus I of Rome (r. 115–25) were revered universally almost from the start, as their cults spread rapidly from one Christian community to another."[3] The early Christians spoke of those who had died for the faith as their "invisible friends."[4]

"We, the Christian community, assemble to celebrate the memory of the martyrs with ritual solemnity," wrote St. Augustine of Hippo (354–430), "because we want to be inspired to follow their example, share in their merits, and be helped by their prayers."[5]

One of the earliest church councils, the Council of Chalcedon, declared in 451 that Flavian "lives after death! May the martyr pray for us!"[6] And the Christian community in Smyrna—today Ismid, Turkey—observed February 23 as the day St. Polycarp died for the faith:

> We have at last gathered his bones, which are dearer than priceless gems and purer than gold, and laid them to rest where it was befitting they should lie. . . . May God grant us to celebrate the birthday of his martyrdom with gladness, thus to recall the memory of those who fought in the glorious combat, and to teach and

strengthen by his example, those who shall come after us.[7]

By the ninth century, *confessors*—persons who were not martyrs but who had witnessed heroically for the faith during their lifetimes—were included among those venerated as saints.

Catholics do not worship saints; only God deserves our worship. We honor the saints, we ask them to pray for us, and we study the stories of their lives on earth—and in some cases their writings—to gather whatever inspiration and wisdom we can. Our purpose on earth is the same as their purpose was, to be faithful disciples of the risen Christ and to share the glad tidings about God's unconditional love for all people and all of creation.

Humans Who Were More Deeply Human

There is one important point we need to keep in mind throughout this entire discussion: *Saints are not sinners who became perfect before they died; rather, saints are human beings whose love for God and neighbor made them more deeply human than the average person.* In other words, the saints show us God, but they also show us what it means to fulfill our humanity.

In not a single case can we say that a saint was a person without personal idiosyncrasies, foibles, or habits that irritated other people. Your average saint sometimes drove other people right up the wall. Your average saint sometimes had bad breath or body odor and made irritating noises while eating. Your average saint was sometimes a narrow-minded, prejudiced person who refused to see other people's points of view. Many people believe that Mother Teresa of Calcutta was a living saint. But talk to the people who knew Mother Teresa best, who rubbed elbows with her on a daily basis, and they will acknowledge that she was not always heaven to live with.

Many saints were perfectly cordial to other people most of the time. But sometimes even these saints were not nice to other people. In the Gospels, sometimes Jesus is not "nice" to other people. Sometimes authentic holiness means *not* being nice. Sometimes speaking out for the truth means not being nice. Sometimes standing up for justice means not being nice.

St. Jerome (c. 341–420) was the greatest Scripture scholar of the early church. All the same, he could be an extremely unpleasant person. A church historian said of St. Jerome, "He was a man of explosive temperament with an uncontrollable, nasty tongue."[8]

Neither are saints without fault from the moment of birth. St. Thérèse of Lisieux (1873–97) is one of the most popular saints of our era, but Thérèse was a spoiled youngest child. When Thérèse was a very young girl, one of her older sisters wrote in a letter that her baby sister "flies into frightful tantrums; when things don't go just right and according to her way of thinking, she rolls on the floor in desperation like one without any hope. There are times when it gets too much for her and she literally chokes."[9]

Neither is it true that during his lifetime a saint was always Mr. Goody Two-Shoes. Take St. Anthony of Padua (1195–1231). "Devotees think of Anthony as sweet and meek," wrote author John Deedy, "but he had a tongue that could blister, particularly as he preached on favorite themes of his: greed and luxurious living, among both lay people and the clergy. Anthony spared no one, not even the mitered [i.e., bishops]. Invited once to preach at a synod at Bourges in central France, he stunned his audience by launching into a denunciation of the presiding prelate, Archbishop Simon de Sully, the very person who had invited him. *Tibi loquor cornute,* he began: 'As for you there, with the miter on your head . . .'"[10]

Sometimes a particular saint's spirituality strikes us today as unbalanced or downright strange. Once again, we need to keep in mind that a saint was a person of his or her own time and place. Historical and cultural differences need to be taken into account. But if we are patient, we will find that the saint's ultimate motivation was love of God and neighbor.

What makes a saint a saint, then? Because each one was an individual, he or she became a saint in a unique fashion. "The saint is a saint," said the great Protestant theologian Paul Tillich, "not because he is 'good' but because he is transparent for something that is more than he himself is."[11] A saint is a person who became transparent to God's love in the world.

We can also see saints as people who did ordinary things with extraordinary care and compassion. A saint may have been certifiably neurotic, but that does not matter. A particular saint's contemporaries may have thought of him or her as a walking nutcase, but that also does not matter.[12] A saint may have been irritable, grouchy, narrow-minded, an all-around pain in the derriere, but that does not matter. What matters is that he or she actually lived as if God's love is real, something that most of us, at best, manage in fits and starts.

Who Becomes a Saint?

For the purposes of this book we will limit our discussion to saints who have been officially recognized as such by the Catholic Church. We do well to acknowledge, however, that there are some twentieth-century personages who have a widespread reputation for saintliness but who have not yet been recognized as saints by the church. Our own theological inclinations are often reflected in who we think should be made a saint. Thus, many conservative Catholics think that Pope Pius XII—the last pope prior to the mid-1960s' reform-minded Second Vatican Council—was a saint, while many progressive Catholics think the same of Pope John XXIII, who convened Vatican II. Other names from our era often mentioned as potential saints include Dorothy Day, co-founder of the Catholic Worker movement; Thomas Merton, Trappist monk and author; Mother Teresa of Calcutta; and Archbishop Oscar Romero of El Salvador, who was murdered by military assassins because he spoke out for the rights of the poor.

A person doesn't become a saint by accident. To *canonize* means to place a person's name in the canon, or list, of saints, and the process that results in an officially canonized Roman Catholic saint is a long and winding road. The notion of "sainthood" or "saintliness" is, of course, not limited to Catholicism. Virtually every religion on the face of the earth has its holy figures, but only the Catholic Church has a formal, institutionalized process to determine if a person is a saint or not. Kenneth L. Woodward offers an explanation of this process:

> To "canonize" means to declare that a person is worthy of universal public cult. Canonization takes place through a solemn papal declaration that a person is, for certain, with God. Because of that certainty, the faithful can, with confidence, pray to the saint to intercede with God on their behalf. The person's name is inscribed in the church's list of saints and he or she is "raised to the altars"—that is, assigned a feast day for liturgical veneration by the entire church.[13]

WHO ARE THE SAINTS?

To put it more concisely: "A saint in the Christian tradition is someone whose holiness is recognized as exceptional by other Christians."[14]

Your grandmother or grandfather may have been a very pious, even saintly, person—one whose faith, hope, and love were regarded by acquaintances as heroic. Unless, however, your grandparent became a public figure, before or after death, don't expect official sainthood to happen. According to the doctrine of the Communion of Saints, you may pray privately to your holy grandparent, asking for prayers on your behalf or on behalf of other loved ones. But devotion to your pious progenitor will almost certainly never become widespread public veneration. Therefore, he or she will never become an officially canonized saint of the Catholic Church.

The official process of canonization has a fascinating history. Although today the process is highly structured, it was not always so. During the first four hundred years of Christian history, pagan Rome's persecution of believers was so common that declaring you were a Christian was the same as announcing your readiness to die for the faith. The early church believed that those who gave their lives for Christ gained eternal life, and the anniversary of a martyr's death was celebrated with joy. Indeed, this belief in eternal life was a unique characteristic of Christianity.

Others who suffered for their faith in Christ but were not executed—called confessors because they publicly "confessed" their faith—were also honored following their eventual death. With the passage of time, Christians who lived an outstanding Christian life, in particular those who practiced great austerity in the spirit of the martyrs, were honored after death in a way similar to martyrs and confessors.

In subsequent centuries, the church honored still other exemplary Christians, including holy bishops, missionaries who carried the gospel to distant lands, virgins (women who never had sexual intercourse and who remained unmarried in order to dedicate themselves entirely to Christ), and doctors of the church (those officially recognized as distinguished teachers of the faith). Still, there was no formal canonization process required for a person to be called a saint.

To make things still more interesting, simple popular opinion could influence who became a saint. Each region proclaimed its own patron saints, and as will happen when popular opinion runs amok, abuses developed. Each region developed its own list of martyrs and confessors, as did each monastery and each nation. In fact, not until the seventeenth century, following the Protestant Reformation, did the church finally establish a single list, or canon, of saints for the whole church.

In some places, ordinary people began to pay more attention to the tombs of the saints, and to their relics, than to the presence of the risen Christ in the Eucharist, or Mass. This trend gave rise to a theological debate. Christ alone was worthy of worship, while the honor accorded to saints was called veneration.

In 410 an official church council, the Council of Carthage, regulated the veneration of saints by insisting that "local bishops should destroy all altars set up as memorials to martyrs and not permit any new shrines to be built unless they contained relics or were established on sites known to be hallowed by the saint's life or death."[15]

From this point on, the devotion of the people remained the spark that would begin a saint's canonization process, but local bishops reserved for themselves the right to declare officially that a person was, indeed, a saint. Before such a declaration could be made, the life of the holy one had to be examined and accounts of alleged miracles studied. Only with the bishop's approval would a feast day be assigned for celebration within the diocese.

Bishops insisted that a written account of the holy person's life be drawn up and witnesses be called. Unfortunately, the written account was often inflated with mere hearsay and purported miracles that could be neither proved nor disproved. Once the bishop gave his approval, however, the alleged saint's body would be moved from its original burial place to an altar in a church or chapel. The installation of the body in an altar came to symbolize the official act of canonization.[16]

All this remained a local matter until about the year 993, when Pope John XV canonized Ulric, the bishop of Augsburg, Germany, who had died in 973. This was the first time a pope canonized a saint, thus giving the whole church's stamp of approval to a local saint.[17] From this time on, the canonization process became more and more formal and institutionalized. By the end of the tenth century there was an increasing conviction throughout the church that only a pope, because he is the ultimate authority in the church, should be allowed to say who was a saint and who was not.

After this, popes got increasingly involved in the saint-making process, intervening in local proceedings when it seemed important for them to do so. Popes began to demand greater assurance that the deceased person was, indeed, exceptionally holy. Alleged miracles had to be proven authentic, and reliable witnesses had to testify to the person's holiness. Pope Urban II (r. 1088–99) said that he would not canonize one Abbot Gurloes unless the monks of his monastery could bring forward eyewitnesses who could swear that they had seen miracles for which the late abbot was supposed to be responsible.

Later, in the 1100s, Pope Alexander III raised holy hell with a bishop for allowing the veneration of a monk who had been dispatched from this life in a drunken brawl. It made no difference to Alexander that local people swore that miracles had happened through the monk's intercession. Monks who got into drunken brawls did not exhibit Alexander's idea of the kind of holiness that people should admire.[18]

The wheels of the church turn slowly, however, and it was not until 1234 that Pope Gregory IX ruled that only saints canonized by papal decree are legitimate. Of course, this did not happen without objections. The more distant a region was from Rome, the more likely the people were to cry foul when the pope issued a decree that would change the way things were done locally.

> In the first place, many saints had long since died and were already the objects of robust local cults. Who was the pope, after all these years, to deny their validity? How, in any case, was he or his legates to conduct a retrospective investigation into the saint's life to determine whether he actually merited the people's veneration?[19]

In the long run, however, the papacy had its way, and centralization of the saint-making process was no doubt a good thing. Oddly enough, it was only during the years when the papacy was temporarily exiled to Avignon, France (1309–77), that an efficient system was established to administer the canonization process. During these years the process became a full-scale judicial procedure. In effect, the candidate was put on trial to determine if he or she was a saint or not. The *prosecutor of the cause* presented as much evidence as he could find in the candidate's favor, while the *promoter of the faith*—popularly known as "the devil's advocate"—brought forward all the negative evidence he could dig up. In addition, the process now required letters from secular and religious authorities asking that a canonization process be started.

The Saint-Making Process

Nearly three hundred years later, in 1512, Pope Julius II established the two-step process of beatification and canonization. Thus, the holy person is first declared to be *blessed,* or *beatified.* After further examination, and after more time has passed, the beatified person may or may not be canonized an official saint of the church.[20]

In 1588 Pope Sixtus V delegated to the Vatican's Sacred Congregation of Rites the responsibility for processing candidates for canonization. Almost four hundred years later, in 1983, Pope John Paul II issued a decree that revised and simplified the canonization process. Harkening back to the early days of the church, John Paul II increased the authority and role of the local bishop in the preliminary determination of candidates for canonization. Today, the Vatican's Congregation for the Causes of Saints is in charge of this process.[21]

As the canonization procedure now operates, a person called a *petitioner,* who personally knew and/or has extensive knowledge of the holy person, writes to the local bishop asking that a particular person be considered for canonization. The bishop then assigns someone called the postulator to investigate the person's life and writings. The *postulator* is an expert in theology, church law, and historical research, plus he or she must be familiar with how things operate in the Congregation for the Causes of Saints.

Once the postulator completes the investigation, he or she writes a biography of the candidate, and this, plus copies of all of the candidate's writings, are sent to the bishop. Along the way, experts investigate any alleged miracles attributed to the prayers of the candidate. These authorities may include medical experts, psychologists, historians, and theologians.

Next, the bishop—or, more likely, someone delegated by the bishop to act in his place—supervises the interviewing of witnesses and a close examination of the candidate's writings. The bishop is also responsible for consulting with other bishops in the region, the Catholic population in general, various experts who may be called to give testimony, and even the pope. Once all this happens, the bishop directs that the collection of documents associated with the case, which are called *The Acts of the Cause,* be boxed up and sent to the Vatican. There, the Congregation for the Causes of Saints reviews the materials.

If the candidate is judged by the Congregation to be worthy, he or she is declared to be *venerable.* At this point, a vigorous investigation of the candidate's life begins in order to find whether he or she showed a heroic degree of what are called the theological and cardinal virtues: faith, hope, love, prudence, justice, fortitude, and temperance. After the Congregation discusses the candidate's merits, evidence must be found for one miracle that may, beyond all doubt, be attributed to the holy person's intercession. An exhaustive scientific and theological study of the alleged miracle must then be completed as proof of God's approval.

Finally, the Congregation presents all the evidence to the pope in a ceremonial setting. If the pope is convinced that the candidate did indeed show heroic holiness, he publishes a declaration that says it is appropriate to venerate the person as truly holy, or *blessed.* From then on, the church refers to the person as "Blessed Steve Barnclapper" or "Blessed Joan Swizzlegroppen."

At a special liturgy of beatification, the pope declares that Blessed Steve or Blessed Joan was a genuinely holy person during his or her lifetime, and therefore the faithful are encouraged to pray to him or her and gather inspiration from his or her example. Still, Blessed Steve and Blessed Joan are not added to the church's universal liturgical calendar. For that, a person must be canonized, and that is the next and final step in the process. A considerable number of candidates for canonization make it no further than beatification, however.

Later, if people attribute further miracles to Blessed Steve or Blessed Joan, the process continues with further investigation to determine whether the miracles are authentic.

If, in the end, the pope determines that the miracles are a result of prayers asking for the intercession of Steve or Joan, he issues a document of canonization declaring that the holy person is a saint. This document recommends veneration of Saint Steve or Saint Joan to the whole church and establishes the new saint's feast day. The canonization is then celebrated at a lengthy, formal ceremony.

The existence of such a church process for canonization may be misleading. The fact is that God, not the church, makes saints. The canonization process exists as a human attempt to make sure that only authentic saints are identified as such. God makes saints. "Still, it is up to us to tell their stories. That, in the end, is the only rationale for the process of 'making saints.'"[22]

Here, then, are some of the saints' stories.

CHAPTER TWO

The Five Most Popular Saints

There are thousands of saints. *The Golden Legend,* the classic medieval collection of mostly legendary stories about saints, includes hundreds of Christian heroes.[1] Butler's *Lives of the Saints,* the classic source for the lives of the saints, runs to four volumes, each nearly two inches thick.[2] John Delaney's one-volume *Dictionary of Saints* includes some five thousand saints and *beati.*[3] *Our Sunday Visitor's Encyclopedia of Saints,* by Matthew Bunson and others, is a book you could use as a doorstop.[4]

There are saints for virtually every nation, culture, and historical period. There are male and female saints, saints who seem to be all sweetness and light, and saints who are curmudgeons. As we shall see in chapter 7, there are patron saints for practically every vocation, profession, trade, and human situation. Finally, while most saints really existed, a few popular saints are legendary at best, though their stories nevertheless have inspirational value.

The saints are a fascinating company of men, women, and children who devoted their lives to Christ and his teachings in widely varied ways.

> They came from every walk of life—from poor peasant tilling his soil to eke out a living and poverty-stricken slum dweller of a large city to emperor and king. Murderers, cutthroats and robbers who repented of their evil lives are listed next to holy men and women who lived lives of holiness and austerity from early childhood. Men, women, and children, black, white, red, yellow, brown, clergy and laity, powerful and helpless, eloquent and tongue-tied—all are represented in this glorious company.[5]

We could populate whole cities with saints. Still, the fact that a saint is a saint does not guarantee his or her ongoing popularity. Some saints sink into obscurity soon after they are canonized. Some are popular only in the corner of the world where they happened to live. Other saints remain an object of great affection and a source of inspiration many centuries after their deaths.

How, then, is one to choose the most popular saints? No matter how objective one may try to be, the process of selection is bound to be affected by subjective influences. The saints I have chosen seem to have staying power. They have remained popular long after they died, and countless people turn to them in prayer, asking for their intercession.

St. Francis of Assisi appeals to the popular imagination for his simplicity and love of creation. Countless people love St. Thérèse of Lisieux because she showed that holiness can happen in the most ordinary, everyday situations. St. Thomas More inspires us because he was a married man and father who became a saint through involvement with worldly affairs, and he did so with courage, humility, and good humor. St. Teresa of Ávila was a strong woman who allowed no one to push her around. Even though she was a great mystic and theologian, St. Teresa's teachings on prayer make sense to ordinary people. Finally, the story of St. Augustine of Hippo is filled with drama that captivates people fifteen hundred years after he lived, and his many theological works are considered among the greatest ever produced.

St. Francis of Assisi

Few would dispute that **Francesco Bernardone (c. 1181–1226)** is probably the most popular saint of all time. Born in Assisi, Italy, the son of wealthy silk merchant Pietro Bernardone, Francis (to use his English name) was baptized Giovanni (John) by his French mother, Donna Pica, who gave birth to him while his father was away on business. When Pietro returned, however, he insisted in no uncertain terms that his son be renamed Francesco. The boy grew up much as the son of any rich man might, able to have anything he wanted and dedicated to a life of pleasure and fun. Francis "grew up a typical spoiled little lord, arrogant and at the same time superficially sociable, the adored center of a noisy band of young people because he had the most money."[6] Today, Francis might be called a party animal.

When Francis was about the age of twenty-one, war broke out between Assisi and the neighboring town of Perugia. Francis and his companions saw this war as an adventure, a welcome diversion from the usual round of partying and carrying on. Pietro Bernardone proudly outfitted his son for battle with the best horse and the best gear that money could buy, but soon after he rode off to war, Francis was taken prisoner and thrown into a cell. Not greatly upset by his circumstances, Francis waited for a year for ransom money to arrive from Assisi. Deprived of his freedom of movement, young Francis had time to think about his future.

How or why Francis decided during this time to change his way of life remains uncertain; legends offer the only explanations we have. Still, it takes little imagination to conjecture that in silence and solitude the grace of God can work wonders. Francis's mother, Donna Pica, seems to have been a woman whose faith was alive and active, and perhaps her influence during Francis's boyhood finally surfaced as the young man lay in prison, waiting.

One legend tells us that, while in prison, Francis decided that upon his release he would join the army of the pope and thus win glory as a soldier. But then, in a dream, a voice said, "Who can give you a better gift, the Lord or the servant? Why are you leaving the Lord for the sake of a servant, and the rich man for a pauper?"[7]

If this story carries any historical value at all, the dream reduced the pope to the status of a mere servant, God being the only one worth serving. This notion of serving only God would later become a major theme of Francis's life. Whatever the ultimate cause of his conversion, when Francis was released a couple of years later, he returned to the war. Francis's biographers tell us that he had a vision of Christ while in the town of Spoleto, then another vision after he returned to Assisi, and he was inspired to make a radical change in his life.

Sometimes a saint's first biographers seem to say that the saint "had a vision" as a way of explaining an inner experience the saint had that we simply cannot know about or understand. To say that the saint had a vision may simply be a way to say that the saint had a profoundly moving religious experience that left him or her a changed person. Regardless, however, the experience that led to Francis's change of heart is not as important as the results of that experience. Francis "dropped out." He lived in a cave and found new friends: lepers, beggars, and the poor. He took his meals with the lepers and cared for them, washing the pus from their sores and forcing himself to kiss their hands. "And when I left them," Francis later wrote, "I found that what had seemed bitter to me was transformed into sweetness."[8]

THE FIVE MOST POPULAR SAINTS

The man who would be called *Il Poverello*, "the Little Poor Man," made a pilgrimage to Rome. When he returned to Assisi, his father announced publicly that his son was a lunatic, and then he disinherited Francis. In a famous scene, Francis disrobed in public, before the bishop of Assisi, giving up all the wealth and privilege he had from his father, and announced that God was his Father. "From now on," he declared, "I will freely say: Our Father in heaven, and no longer: Father Pietro Bernardone. I want to go to heaven naked."[9]

In the countryside near Assisi, Francis came upon the tumbledown church of San Damiano, where he found a unique and captivating Roman-Byzantine-style crucifix, the image of which is now famous and reproduced widely. Francis liked to spend time before this crucifix in prayer, and today the very crucifix Francis prayed before hangs in the Basilica of St. Clare, in Assisi.

According to the story passed down for more than seven hundred years, one day as the young Francis prayed before this crucifix, seeking knowledge of what to do with his life, he clearly heard a voice that said, "Francis, go and restore my house; it's falling apart, as you see." Thinking the voice spoke of the church of San Damiano, Francis gathered about him several companions, also seeking to do God's will, and together they began to repair the little church. To earn money for building materials, Francis walked from village to village, singing in the marketplaces.

Later, in another abandoned chapel called the *Portiun-cula,* "Little Portion," Francis had a life-changing experience. A wandering priest stopped by and celebrated the Eucharist. He read from the Gospel of Matthew: "As you go, proclaim the good news, 'The kingdom of heaven has come near.' . . . You received without payment; give without payment. Take no gold, or silver, or copper in your belts, no bag for your journey, or two tunics, or sandals, or a staff" (10:7–10).

You could have knocked Francis over with a goose feather. He knew that this was what he wanted. With all his heart, this was how he wanted to live. Francis's first bio-grapher, Thomas of Celano, says that at this point Francis gave away his shoes, donned the simple garb of a mountain shepherd, traded his leather belt for a length of rope—and this was the beginning of the Franciscan habit.

It is important to keep in mind that surely Francis's experience could not have been as smooth and relatively uncomplicated as the story seems. Pietro Bernardone must have tried every way he could to reclaim his son from the insanity that seemed to have seized him. There must have been many unpleasant encounters between father and son. Francis stands as something of a patron saint for young people who rebel against parents in an attempt to follow a different drummer.

Within a few years, Francis had established himself with a few companions, and together they walked the Umbrian countryside begging for their food and talking with people about the good news of Jesus, the risen Lord. Many called Francis crazy, but sometimes they liked what he said about peace. Some even appreciated Francis's call to repentance and conversion. In at least one case a wealthy man, Bernardo of Quintavalle, sold all his possessions and joined Francis's troop of friends. Others joined as well, including a knight, a peasant, a poet named Guglielmo Divini, a huge man Francis called Brother Masseo, and a not-terribly-bright, but good-hearted chap Francis named Brother Juniper. The brothers lived together in barns or old chapels, and they promised one another that they would follow the gospel in every aspect of their life with Francis.

Later in life, when Francis's original vision was being questioned, he would recall how he and the first Franciscans lived:

> Those who came and adopted this life gave everything they had to the poor. They were content with a single cowl, patched inside and out, with a staff and under-wear. We had no wish to have any more than that.
>
> . . . We were uneducated and subject to everyone. I worked with my hands and I want to continue doing so, and I wish all the other brothers to do honest work. Whoever doesn't know how must learn. . . . When we get no pay, let us take refuge at the table of the Lord and beg for alms from door to door.[10]

The early Franciscans did not support themselves entirely by begging. In their wanderings they worked for farmers or in houses where people with leprosy lived.

In 1210 Francis received from Pope Innocent III verbal approval for the simple rule he had drawn up. Two years later, Francis was joined by the first woman Franciscan, Clare, who arrived in spite of the violent objections of her family. (Clare's story, too, is the stuff of legends and deserves the reader's attention.)

Francis became known for his love of the natural world. Stories circulated about Francis's preaching a sermon to the birds. Another story told of how Francis tamed a vicious wolf near the town of Gubbio. These stories were collected in a volume called *The Little Flowers of St. Francis.*[11]

Determined to preach the gospel to the Muslims, Francis boarded a ship for Syria in 1212, but the journey ended in shipwreck. A second attempt also ended in failure when Francis, on his way to Morocco, became ill in Spain and had to return to Italy. Finally, in 1219, the membership of his order having grown to some five thousand, Francis made it to Egypt with twelve of his brothers. Even though he met with Sultan Malek al-Kamil, Francis's mission was a failure. However, the sultan recognized Francis as a holy man, so he did not allow anyone to harm him.

Hearing of a movement within his order to water down his original simple rule of life, Francis returned with an appointment from the Vatican as the official protector of the

Franciscan order. With this authority, in 1221 he was able to maintain, for the time being, the simple ideals upon which the Franciscan life had been founded. A few years later, however, another uprising in the order was more successful, and the Franciscan life became less harsh.

By 1223 Francis had handed over the practical direction of the order to Brother Elias, the man who would be his successor and who was also in favor of lightening the burden Francis's original rule placed on the brothers. That Christmas, Francis visited the little town of Gréccio, and he directed the building of the first crèche, or Nativity scene, thus establishing a custom that remains popular all over the Christian world to this day.

The following year, Francis retired to a hermitage on Mount Alvernia, and while at prayer on September 14, 1224, he received the *stigmata*—the wounds of Christ in hands, feet, and side—in his own body. Soon thereafter, Francis returned to the Portiuncula. During this time, near the end of his life, Francis wrote his most famous song, "Canticle of Brother Sun," which begins, "Most High Almighty, Good Lord, / Yours are praise, glory, honor and all blessing. / To you alone, Most High, do they belong, / And no man is worthy to mention You. / Be praised, my Lord, with all Your creatures, / Especially Sir Brother Sun, / Who is daylight, and by him You shed light on us."[12]

The Little Poor Man died two years later. Sensing that he was near death, he asked the brothers present to lay him naked on the ground that he might welcome Sister Death in complete poverty. Not long before he died, Francis added a final verse to his "Canticle of Brother Sun": "Be praised my Lord, for our Sister Bodily Death, / From whom no living man can escape. . . ."[13]

Francis died singing, literally. Lying naked on the ground, he chanted Psalm 142: "I cried to the Lord with my voice: with my voice I made supplication to the Lord."[14]

Four years after his death, Francis was canonized a saint. He was never ordained a priest, believing himself unworthy of the priesthood, although he does seem to have received ordination as a deacon. Down through the centuries, Francis has had a tremendous impact on the faith and lives of Christians the world over. "His life was characterized by joyous worship, reverence for nature, and concern for the sick and poor. He is depicted in liturgical art in his habit, with the stigmata, and sometimes with a winged crucifix. He is also depicted giving sermons to animals or birds."[15]

The feast day of St. Francis is October 4.

St. Thérèse of Lisieux

Thérèse Martin (1873–97) is one of the most popular and enigmatic saints of all time, and because she lived in the late nineteenth century we have more information about her than about many saints from earlier eras. Many photographs of her survive and have been published.

29

Marie Françoise Thérèse[16] was born January 2, 1873, in Alençon, France. She was the youngest of nine children, five of whom survived infancy. Her mother, Zélie Guerin Martin, died from breast cancer when Thérèse was five. Her father, Louis Martin, was an affluent watchmaker who provided his family with a comfortable upper-middle-class life. After his wife's death, Louis moved the family to Lisieux, where Thérèse was brought up by two older sisters and an aunt. Little Thérèse was fawned over and spoiled by everyone—she was the poor little thing whose mother had died.

When Thérèse was still a young girl, her oldest sister, Pauline, became a Carmelite nun. Later, when Thérèse was fourteen, her sister Marie followed. On Christmas Eve of that year, Thérèse had an experience she later referred to as her "conversion." She described it thus: "On that blessed night the sweet child Jesus, scarcely an hour old, filled the darkness of my soul with floods of light. By becoming weak and little, for love of me, He made me strong and brave; He put His own weapons into my hands so that I went on from strength to strength, beginning, if I may say so, 'to run as a giant.'"[17]

During the following year, Thérèse told her father that she, too, wanted to become a Carmelite nun. Louis Martin reluctantly agreed, but both the mother superior of the Carmelites and the bishop of Bayeux—the diocese in which the Martins were living—put the kibosh on that idea because Thérèse was only fourteen years old.

A few months later, Thérèse was in Rome with her father, on a pilgrimage in honor of a papal jubilee. At a public audience with Pope Leo XIII, each pilgrimage participant was allowed to approach the pope for a blessing. When her turn came, Thérèse impulsively knelt before the pope and broke the traditional rule of silence on such occasions. "In honor of your jubilee," she begged, "allow me to enter Carmel at fifteen."[18]

Clearly impressed by this young girl, Leo XIII nevertheless told Thérèse to obey the mother superior and the bishop. "You shall enter if it be God's will," he said kindly.[19]

At the end of that year, the bishop gave his permission, and the following spring, on April 9, 1888, Thérèse Martin entered the Carmelite monastery in Lisieux to join her two older sisters. "From her entrance," her novice mistress later reported, "she surprised the community by her bearing, which was marked by a certain dignity that one would not expect in a child of fifteen."[20]

One reason that devotion to St. Thérèse seems to be so healthy is that she had a great familiarity with Scripture. Her autobiographical classic, *Story of a Soul,* is filled with biblical quotations.[21] She was also deeply devoted to liturgical prayer, clearly understanding that the Mass is, to use the traditional phrase, the "source and summit" of the Christian life. Thus, by her example St. Thérèse encourages those devoted to her to love both Scripture and the liturgy as the heart of a deeply Christian spirituality.

THE FIVE MOST POPULAR SAINTS

In 1889 Louis Martin suffered a series of strokes and had to be cared for in a private facility for three years prior to his death. His mind was affected, so he no longer recognized loved ones. Thérèse had a deeply spiritual grasp of these years that we may find difficult to understand. She said, "The three years of my father's martyrdom seem to me the dearest and most fruitful of our life. I would not exchange them for the most sublime ecstasies."[22]

We live in an era when Louis Martin, in his debilitated condition, would seem an ideal candidate for euthanasia. Instead, Thérèse reminds us of the mystery of suffering from a Christian perspective. Blessings come from suffering we do not seek, both for those who suffer and for those who care for the one who suffers so mysteriously. Euthanasia, then, is a merely utilitarian way to avoid inconvenience, as if human suffering were no mystery at all but a bother and a scandal for which a technological solution must be found and used.

Thérèse took her first vows as a Carmelite nun on September 8, 1890. "The autobiography which [Thérèse] wrote at the command of her prioress, *L'histoire d'une âme [Story of a Soul],* is a unique and engaging document, written with a delightful clarity and freshness, full of surprising turns of phrase, bits of unexpected knowledge and unconscious self-revelation, and, above all, of deep spiritual wisdom and beauty."[23]

For example, in a single, somewhat naive, sentence in which Thérèse addresses God in a most surprising manner, considering her nineteenth-century bourgeois French up-bringing, she states with great simplicity the profound mystery of human existence. Her name for God sounds like something from a book on New Age spirituality or the work of someone trying to imitate Native American religion: "Eternal Eagle, you desire to nourish me with your divine substance, and yet I am but a poor little thing who would return to nothingness if Your divine glance did not give me life from one moment to the next."[24]

The heart of St. Thérèse's spirituality is her "little way," a spirituality that sees holiness in the most ordinary, obscure tasks and human interactions. While Thérèse's piety sometimes strikes the modern reader as too sweetly sentimental, she found the essence of her "little way" spirituality in three Old Testament verses: "Whoever is a little one, let him come to me" (Proverbs 9:4); "For to him that is little, mercy will be shown" (Wisdom 6:7); "As one whom a mother caresses, so will I comfort you; you shall be carried at the breasts, and upon the knees they shall fondle you" (Isaiah 66:12–13).[25]

St. Thérèse is often called the Little Flower, a name she used for herself in her autobiography. This nickname may also strike the modern reader as unattractively sentimental. Again, however, if we look closely at what Thérèse actually wrote, the name seems not sentimental at all:

> Just as the sun shines simultaneously on the tall cedars and on each little flower as though it were alone on the

earth, so Our Lord is occupied particularly with each soul as though there were no others like it. And just as in nature all the seasons are arranged in such a way as to make the humblest daisy bloom on a set day, in the same way, everything works out for the good of each soul.[26]

When Thérèse called herself a "little flower," she used the image to convey not weakness but strength, much as St. Paul does: "Therefore I am content with weaknesses, insults, hardships, persecutions, and calamities for the sake of Christ; for whenever I am weak, then I am strong" (2 Corinthians 12:10).

Thérèse also had a perfectly ideal and perfectly simple understanding of prayer when she wrote, "I do as a child who has not learned to read—I just tell our Lord all that I want and He understands."[27]

In 1893 Thérèse, only twenty years old, was directed to be assistant to the novice mistress. In fact, however, she was novice mistress herself in all but the official title. She wrote, "From afar it seems easy to do good to souls, to make them love God more, to mold them according to our own ideas and views. But coming closer we find, on the contrary, that to do good without God's help is as impossible as to make the sun shine at night."[28]

Following the death of Louis Martin in 1894, Thérèse's sister Céline also entered the Lisieux convent. A year and a half later, during the night, Thérèse realized that she had contracted tuberculosis, and the last eighteen months of her life were filled with physical suffering and spiritual difficulty. The spirit of prophecy seemed to come upon her, and it was now that she made those three utterances that have gone round the world: "I have never given the good God aught but love, and it is with love that He will repay. After my death I will let fall a shower of roses." "I will spend my Heaven in doing good upon earth." "My 'little way' is the way of spiritual childhood, the way of trust and absolute self-surrender."[29]

In June 1897 Thérèse was moved into the convent infirmary, and September 30 was her last day on earth. One of her biographers described the scene thus:

> In the afternoon the end seemed near and the nuns assembled but after two hours were sent away again. "Am I not to die yet?" Thérèse asked. "Very well, let it be so. I do not wish to suffer less."
>
> At seven in the evening, the nuns were again summoned. Gazing at her crucifix, Thérèse said, "Oh, I love Him. My God, I love you" and died. The photograph taken after death shows a face beautiful, young, and peaceful.[30]

Following her death, Thérèse's sisters decided to publish the notebooks she had filled with her thoughts and memories. Within two years, five thousand copies had been sold. Thérèse quickly gained a popularity unmatched by any candidate for sainthood in modern times. A young French seminarian suffering from tuberculosis was cured instantly after praying for Thérèse's intercession, and that was but the first of many miracles attributed to her prayers. On May 17, 1925, Thérèse Martin was canonized a saint by Pope Pius XI in St. Peter's Basilica in Rome.

> The basilica was decorated with garlands of roses. It was packed—it was thought there were about sixty thousand people in the congregation, and the square outside was jammed with pilgrims. Mass was said, and the banner of the new saint was carried down the aisle. A few rose petals fell mysteriously from the ceiling during the course of the ceremonies.[31]

St. Thérèse's feast day is October 1.

St. Thomas More

Few saints have captured the popular imagination as thoroughly as **Thomas More (1478–1535).** In contemporary times, *A Man for All Seasons,* the 1960s play and film based on his story, attracted widespread attention to a saint who was a layman, a husband, and a father, and whose holiness expressed itself entirely in the public forum.

Thomas was born in London on February 6, 1478. His father was John More, a lawyer and judge. At the age of twelve, Thomas became a page in the household of John Morton, archbishop of Canterbury. Later he attended Oxford University and studied law at Lincoln's Inn. He was admitted to the bar in 1501 and became a member of Parliament in 1504.

A man of deep faith and attracted to the monastic life, Thomas gave the hermit Carthusians a serious try—he lived with them for four years—but decided instead to marry, which he did in 1505. His wife was Jane Colt, and their home became a center of medieval and Renaissance culture in England. More became one of the leading intellectual figures of his time, much respected for his wisdom, intellectual abilities, and sense of humor.

Thomas More became one of his country's leading humanists and scholars. He wrote poetry, history, and essays in which he debated the Protestant point of view. He also wrote prayers, devotional books, and translations of Latin classics. His great work, *Utopia*, published in 1515, is the story of an imaginary society governed by reason. Another book, *Vindication of Henry against Luther* (1523), is a lively defense of King Henry VIII, whom More had tutored as a boy.

In 1510 More became undersheriff of London. The following year, his first wife, Jane Colt, died suddenly, and a month later Thomas married a widow seven years older than he, Alice Middleton. While he certainly cared for Alice, clearly he needed help with his three young daughters and one son.

After Henry became king, he sent More on diplomatic missions—to France and Flanders—then in 1517 made him a member of the Royal Council. So pleased was Henry with

More's work that he made him a knight in 1521. Two years later, Sir Thomas became speaker of the House of Commons, and two years after that he replaced Cardinal Wolsey as lord chancellor. More had serious doubts about King Henry's wisdom when Henry defied the pope by divorcing Catherine of Aragon, but More remained silent about his feelings. But he also refused to sign a petition to the pope asking permission for Henry to divorce Catherine.

Sir Thomas finally resigned the chancellorship on May 16, 1532, after objecting to a series of rulings against the church. The king wanted to forbid the clergy any power to oppose heretics, and he wanted them to obtain his permission before scheduling any meetings. Henry then introduced a bill in Parliament to keep from the Vatican its traditional income from English bishoprics. Thomas openly opposed all of these measures, angering Henry greatly.

Without the chancellorship, More had no income, and he was reduced to virtual poverty. He returned to his home in Chelsea to write and live quietly. More gathered his family and his greatly reduced household staff around him, and he explained the situation with wry humor. His statement ended, "Then may we yet with bags and wallets go a-begging together, and hoping that for pity some good folk will give us their charity, at every man's door to sing '*Salve regina*,' and so still keep company and be merry together."[32]

For the next eighteen months, Thomas lived a quiet, simple life and occupied himself with writing. He refused to attend the coronation of Anne Boleyn after Henry married her, and More's enemies continued to harass him at every opportunity. They implicated More in trumped-up legal cases, but Henry withdrew the charges.

On March 30, 1534, the Act of Succession required the king's subjects to take an oath recognizing succession to the throne by the offspring of Henry and his second wife, Anne Boleyn. Later, Henry supplemented the document with the information that his marriage with Catherine of Aragon had not been a true marriage, while his marriage to Anne was a true marriage. He also added articles that rejected the authority of "any foreign authority, prince or potentate."[33]

Henry declared that to oppose the Act of Succession would be high treason. Just one week earlier, Pope Clement VII had pronounced the marriage of Henry and his first wife, Catherine, to be valid. Sir Thomas More and John Fisher, bishop of Rochester, were asked to sign the Act of Succession on April 13, and both announced that they would not do so. More was placed in the custody of the abbot of Westminster, and one of Henry's closest advisers urged Henry to compromise, but he refused. More was again presented with the Act of Succession; again he said he would not sign it, and he was immediately imprisoned in the Tower of London—illegally, as it turned out, for the law did not provide for such a punishment.

Sir Thomas More spent the next fifteen months in the Tower. He did so, according to all reports, with remarkable peace of mind given the injustice to which he was a victim. He also showed time and again his tender love for his eldest daughter, Margaret. His letters to Margaret survive, and some of their conversations were recorded. On one occasion, More remarked, "I thank God, Meg, to reckon myself in worse case here than at home, for methinks God maketh me a wanton and setteth me on His lap and dandleth me."[34]

Thomas More's family made every effort to get him to compromise his position with King Henry, but their efforts came to nothing. Henry tightened the screws by making More's imprisonment more difficult. He declared that More was to be allowed no visitors. More responded with equanimity and began to write his *Dialogue of Comfort against Tribulation,* which scholars agree is the best of his spiritual works.

In November, Thomas was deprived of virtually all that he owned. Except for a small pension given by the Order of St. John of Jerusalem, he and his family were penniless. His wife, Alice, had to sell some of her clothes to provide Thomas with a few necessities. Twice she petitioned King Henry to have pity and release her husband, but Henry refused.

On February 1, 1535, the Act of Supremacy became effective. The decree gave the king the title of "only supreme head of the Church of England" and made it treason to deny this. When asked his opinion of the Act of Supremacy, Thomas More declined to give one. On May 4, More and his daughter, who was visiting him for the last time, watched as three Carthusian monks climbed the scaffold to die. "Lo!"

More exclaimed. "Dost thou not see, Meg, that these blessed fathers be now as cheerfully going to their deaths as bridegrooms to their marriage? . . . Whereas thy silly father, Meg, that like a most wicked caitiff hath passed forth the whole course of his miserable life most sinfully, God, thinking him not so worthy so soon to come to that eternal felicity, leaveth him here yet still in the world further to be plagued and turmoiled with misery."[35]

A few days later, More was again interrogated and taunted for remaining silent. On June 19 three more Carthusian monks were executed, and on June 22 More's old friend Bishop John Fisher was beheaded. More was accused of treason and tried nine days later. False evidence was given, to which More replied in words that ring down through the centuries: "Ye must understand that, in things touching conscience, every true and good subject is more bound to have respect to his said conscience and to his soul than to any other thing in all the world beside."[36]

Thomas More was found guilty and condemned to death. Only then did he speak what he truly believed. He denied that any earthly lord or king could ever dictate to another's spirituality, concluding that even as Paul had persecuted Stephen "and yet be they now both twain holy saints in Heaven, and shall continue there friends for ever, so I verily trust, and shall therefore right heartily pray, that though your lordships have now here on earth been judges of my condemnation, we may yet hereafter in Heaven merrily all meet together to everlasting salvation."[37]

On July 6 Thomas said that he would pray for the king. He put on his best clothes, walked calmly to Tower Hill, and climbed to the scaffold with a joke for the executioner: "I pray you, master Lieutenant, see me safe up, and as for my coming down, let me shift for myself."[38]

More then asked the people to pray for him, declared that he died for the holy Catholic Church, and said that he was "the king's good servant—but God's first." He recited Psalm 51, the *Miserere:* "Have mercy on me, O God, according to your steadfast love; according to your abundant mercy blot out my transgressions. . . ." Finally, More embraced and encouraged his executioner.

Having laid his head on the block, More had time for a final jest. He carefully moved aside the long beard he had grown in prison, explaining to the executioner with a smile, "This hath not offended the king."[39] He was beheaded with a single stroke at the age of fifty-seven.

Thomas More was beatified in 1886 and canonized a saint in 1935. Whether he had died a martyr or not, More would have been reckoned a holy man, one who lived his faith in the everyday world of home, family, work, and career. As such, he stands as an excellent patron for people of faith in our own time.

The feast day of St. Thomas More is June 22.

St. Teresa of Ávila

Even the most traditional of sources on the saints can hardly restrain itself when it talks about **Teresa of Ávila (1515–82),** calling her "one of the greatest, most attractive and widely appreciated women whom the world has ever known."[40] Another author pegs the sixteenth-century Spanish Carmelite nun "a high-spirited bundle of energy, vehement, unbending, always inclined to extremes, a restless soul."[41]

Born in or near Ávila in Castile, Spain, on March 28, 1515, Teresa was the daughter of Don Alonso Sánchez de Cepeda and his second wife, Doña Beatrice Davila y Ahumada. Teresa's paternal grandfather, Juan Sánchez de Toledo, seems to have been a Jewish convert to Catholicism. Don Alonso, a wealthy man, had three children from his first marriage, which ended with the death of his wife, and Beatrice bore him nine more. Teresa later remarked that all her siblings, "through the goodness of God, were like our parents in being virtuous, except myself."

When she was only seven years old, Teresa enjoyed reading about the lives of the saints. She and a brother named Rodrigo, who was near her age, played together and spent much time discussing the saints and their courage. One of the best-known stories from Teresa's childhood recounts the time she and Rodrigo resolved to travel to "the country of the Moors" where they hoped, like the saints of old, to die for their faith. Before they got very far, however, their frantic

THE FIVE MOST POPULAR SAINTS

mother sent an uncle to retrieve them, "whereupon Rodrigo laid all the blame on his sister."[42]

When Teresa was fourteen, her mother died, and Teresa grieved deeply, praying before an image of the Blessed Virgin Mary, asking Mary to become her mother. About this same time, Teresa and Rodrigo began to spend many hours each day reading the romance novels of the time and trying to write some themselves.

"These tales," Teresa later wrote in her autobiography, "did not fail to cool my good desires, and were the cause of my falling insensibly into other defects. I was so enchanted that I could not be content if I had not some new tale in my hands. I began to imitate the fashions, to take delight in being well dressed, to have great care of my hands, to make use of perfumes, and to affect all the vain trimmings which my position in the world allowed."[43]

Teresa's father was so startled by the change in her behavior that he became concerned, so he placed his fifteen-year-old daughter in a convent of Augustinian nuns, where many young women of her social status received an education. Eighteen months later, Teresa came down with a mysterious illness and returned home, where she began to think seriously about entering the religious life. When Teresa told her father that she wished to become a nun, Don Alonso refused to give his consent, saying that after his death she could do whatever she wished.

At the age of twenty, however, Teresa was so determined that she secretly left her father's house at night and went to the Convent of the Incarnation of the Carmelite nuns outside Ávila, where her good friend Sister Jane Suarez lived. Although she felt great anguish at leaving her father and her friends, Teresa went ahead with her plans to become a nun. When Don Alonso learned what his daughter had done, he decided not to oppose her any further.

Teresa, for her part, did not enter the religious life without mixed feelings. She struggled with herself about whether to remain "in the world" or become a nun. Even when she decided to join the Carmelites, she did so for less than the purest of motives. "She seems no longer to have thought herself capable of a life close to God in 'the world.' And so out of an anxious, private faith, she sought the seclusion of the convent: God and my soul, and nothing else. Teresa herself says: 'More than love, slavish fear drove me to take the veil.'"[44]

A year after entering the Convent of the Incarnation, Teresa took her religious vows in spite of having contracted an illness. After taking her vows, this illness grew worse—it is possible that she had malaria—so she returned once again to the home of her father, this time in the company of her friend Sister Jane Suarez. The physicians Don Alonso brought in to treat his daughter were no help, however. The doctors threw up their hands in despair, and Teresa grew even more ill. Finally, after three years, she recovered.

Between 1555 and 1556 Teresa experienced visions and heard heavenly voices, a phenomenon that caused her great anguish because she did not think these experiences were genuine. Then, in 1557 her spiritual director, a Jesuit who would himself become a saint, Peter of Alcántara, helped her to see that such experiences were from God.

In 1562, in the face of tremendous opposition, Teresa founded a new convent, named for St. Joseph, in Ávila. This was a convent for nuns who wished to live a dedicated, fervent religious life rather than the relaxed lifestyle that had turned other convents into centers of socializing for both nuns and ladies of the surrounding community. A married sister of Teresa's, Doña Juana de Ahumada, and her husband built the new convent, but in order to prevent vandalism from those who opposed the new convent, they built it so that it appeared to be a home they were building for themselves.

Teresa's sister and her husband had a little boy, Gonzalez, who, while playing around the construction of the new convent, was accidentally crushed when a wall fell on him. The boy was taken immediately to Teresa, who took him in her arms and prayed for him, and after a while he recovered completely.

The new convent was established with a rule of strict silence and poverty, and the nuns were to spend their time in prayer and household work. When the prior general of the Carmelites, John Baptist Rubeo, visited in 1567, he was impressed with what he saw. He gave Teresa authority to found other convents, even though St. Joseph's had been founded without his knowledge or approval. He even gave Teresa permission to found two Carmelite houses for men in Castile.

During the years when she was establishing new foundations, Teresa also wrote some of the great classics of mystical literature, including her *Autobiography* (1565), *The Way of Perfection* (1573), and *Interior Castle* (1577). "One of the great mystics of all times, she was intelligent, hardheaded, charming, deeply spiritual, and successfully blended a highly active life with a life of deep contemplation."[45]

Teresa had no qualms about standing up to authority figures. When her provincial, Father Angel, questioned her decisions, she responded, "Beware of fighting against the Holy Ghost."[46] In fact, one of Teresa's most attractive attributes was her ability to respect what we call "the institutional church," its leaders and its laws, and at the same time distinguish between such institutional Catholicism and the living Catholic tradition. She knew that we cannot separate the two, but she also knew that for our spiritual health it is necessary to distinguish between them. Teresa could argue with and oppose church authorities when they gave her trouble.

After years of bitter disputes, Pope Gregory XIII finally gave his approval in 1580 to the rule Teresa had written for the communities in her Carmelite reform. Teresa breathed a huge sigh of relief: "Now we are all in good peace . . . and nothing disturbs us in God's service any more."[47]

At the heart of Teresa's mysticism is the warmest and most everyday notion that God is our friend, not some distant, forbidding Supreme Being. Teresa often referred to God as "Majesty," according him the greatest respect, of course. But she also called God "chosen lover" and "good friend." For Teresa, the correct way to pray was to approach God on intimate terms. For her, prayer was simply "a conversation with a friend, with whom we get together often and gladly, so as to talk with Him, because we are sure that He loves us."[48]

Teresa's advice on prayer was both realistic and inspirational. "Accustom yourselves always to have Jesus with you," she declared. The only thing that matters in prayer, she said, is to spend a few minutes with God, even if we are "full of a thousand disturbing cares and worldly thoughts." She also advised against a kind of spiritual athleticism. "It is enough for God if we pray just one Our Father in an hour. The important thing is to think that He is near us."[49]

In her teachings on prayer, Teresa was perfectly in tune with the gospel. "We can't tell whether we love God," she said, "but people can see whether we love our neighbor." For Teresa, prayer should bear fruit in good works: "If you know that you could obtain relief for a sick person, then drop your devotions at once and do it!"[50]

By 1580, when the dispute between the two groups of Carmelites was finally resolved, Teresa was sixty-five years old, her health poor. All the same, in the next two years she founded two more convents, bringing the total to seventeen.

These foundations were made as homes for contemplative Carmelites, but Teresa saw them also as making up for some of the many monasteries and convents destroyed by Protestantism, which was then in its first fervent enthusiasm throughout Europe.

When Teresa's brother Don Lorenzo died, Teresa was—against her own wishes—involved in the legal proceedings. When a lawyer was rude to her, she replied, "Sir, may God return to you the courtesy you have shown me."[51] About this same time, Teresa made her last foundation, at Burgos, in July 1582. Knowing that her life was almost over, Teresa asked to return to Ávila, but her companions talked her into traveling instead to Alba de Tormes, where her friend Duchess Maria Henriquez waited for a visit. Teresa was so ill on the journey that she fainted along the way. When they finally arrived, Teresa went directly to bed. Three days later, she said to one of her companions, "At last, my daughter, the hour of death has come."

A priest friend asked Teresa where she wished to be buried. She replied, "Is it for me to say? Will they deny me a little ground for my body here?" When the Blessed Sacrament was brought to her, Teresa sat up, difficult though it was for her, and exclaimed, "Oh my Lord, now is the time that we may see each other!"[52] She begged her weeping sisters to forgive the "bad example" she had given them.[53]

Then, with a cheerful face, Teresa died. It was October 4, 1582, and she was buried at the convent of Alba de Tormes.

Teresa was canonized a saint a mere forty years later, in 1622. Her writings are read to this day by countless Christians, and some seventeen thousand women and men live according to her rule in twelve hundred convents and monasteries around the world. In 1970 Pope Paul VI made St. Teresa, along with St. Catherine of Siena, one of the first two women doctors of the church, a title given since the Middle Ages to authors of outstanding holiness whose writings have made a significant contribution to the cause of Christ in his church.[54]

St. Teresa's feast day is October 15.

St. Augustine of Hippo

Few saints have a personal story as dramatic as **Augustine of Hippo (354–430).** Augustine was born November 13, 354, in Tagaste, a small town in North Africa not far from Hippo, in modern-day Algeria. Augustine's father, Patricius, a Roman official, was not baptized a Christian until just before his death, and he seems to have had a violent temper. Augustine's mother, Monica, a devout Christian, bore several children of whom we know only two. In his writings, Augustine mentions a brother and a sister.[55]

As a child, Augustine received instruction in the Christian faith from his mother, and she taught him to pray. It was the custom to delay baptism as long as possible in order to avoid sin after being baptized, a custom Augustine rightly deplored in his later writings. Most of what we know of Augustine's early life comes from his famous *Confessions,* the first book ever written in the first-person viewpoint and a major classic of Western literature to this day. Augustine says that he wrote this book for "a people curious to know the lives of others, but careless to amend their own."[56]

Augustine tells us that he attended school as a boy, but he was not an enthusiastic student. "He accuses himself of often studying only by constraint, disobeying his parents and masters, not writing, reading, or minding his lessons so much as was required of him; and this he did not for want of wit or memory, but out of love of play."[57]

In 370, at the age of seventeen, Augustine went to Carthage, where he attended the university to study rhetoric and become a lawyer. There he abandoned his Christian faith. He took a mistress with whom he lived for fifteen years and with whom he fathered a son named Adeodatus, born in 372. It was in Carthage, too, that Augustine became interested in philosophy and embraced Manichaeism, a doctrine that borrowed from Christianity and various Eastern religions. Manichaeism taught a strict asceticism that would liberate the spark of light in human beings and deliver them from matter, which was believed to be evil, and from the darkness of life in this world.[58]

After teaching rhetoric in Tagaste and Carthage for nine years, Augustine met Faustus, the leading Manichaean teacher, and became disillusioned with Manichaeism. Moving to Rome in 383 — secretly, so that his mother, Monica, would not hinder his departure—he soon left there for Milan, where he was well received. The local bishop, Ambrose, liked the young Augustine, and Augustine appreciated Ambrose because of his learning and reputation. Ambrose was widely respected as a preacher, and Augustine began to attend his sermons to satisfy his curiosity and enjoy Ambrose's eloquence.

Augustine found Ambrose to be much better informed and better educated than Faustus, and Ambrose began to make an impression on Augustine. During this time, Augustine also read the works of the Greek philosophers Plato and Plotinus. Also, Monica had followed her son to Milan, and Augustine's former mistress returned to North Africa, leaving Adeodatus behind. During this time Augustine's sexual promiscuity continued.

Eventually, Augustine became convinced of the truth of the Christian faith, but he found himself unable to abandon his old way of life. Augustine prayed, "Give me chastity and continence, but not right away!"[59]

With time, however, Augustine became disgusted with himself, and following a conversation with a friend about the conversion of St. Antony of Egypt, Augustine went into the garden behind his house, his inner turmoil almost too much to bear. Why could he not choose to embrace faith in Christ? Why did he continue to hesitate? "How long? How long? Tomorrow, tomorrow? Why not now?"[60]

Augustine began to weep, his heart aching with sadness, when all of a sudden he heard what seemed to be the voice of a child singing from a nearby house, repeating these words: "Take up and read! Take up and read!" Augustine tried to think of any children's game in which these words would be sung, but he could think of none. He decided that the words were from God. Returning to his friend, who had a copy of the letters of St. Paul, he opened the book and read the first words he saw: "Let us live honorably as in the day, not in reveling and drunkenness, not in debauchery and licentiousness, not in quarreling and jealousy. Instead, put on the Lord Jesus Christ, and make no provision for the flesh, to gratify its desires" (Romans 13:13–14).

Immediately, all reluctance left Augustine. It was September 386, and he was thirty-two years old. At once, he gave up teaching and moved to a house borrowed from a friend, in the countryside near Milan. With him went his mother; his son, Adeodatus, now about seventeen years old; his brother, Navigius; and several friends. He and his small community of friends and loved ones adopted a life of prayer and study. Not long after this, Adeodatus died, much to Augustine's sadness.

Bishop Ambrose baptized Augustine at the Easter Vigil in 387, along with the other members of his household. A few months later, Augustine decided to return to North Africa, his mother and a few other people accompanying him. He sold his father's estate, gave the proceeds to the poor, and moved to yet another rural retreat to live a life of prayer and study. In November of that year, Monica died.

THE FIVE MOST POPULAR SAINTS

Before long, knowledge of Augustine's return and conversion became common knowledge in the vicinity. One day a group of churchgoers came to his door, literally dragged him into the city, and made him promise to accept ordination to the priesthood. So much for a quiet life in the countryside.

Augustine was ordained a priest in 391 and appointed as assistant to the old bishop of Hippo, Valerius. The bishop was Greek, plus he had a speech impediment, so he directed Augustine to take over all the responsibilities for preaching. Augustine encouraged the people to have a realistic view of the church, reminding them that they should not be enthusiastic about the "tremendous Christians" while trying to hush up the "evil mixed in."[61]

The new priest began to publicly oppose the Manichaeans, as well as other groups who were beginning to sprout up with off-the-wall ideas. He also instituted various reforms such as forbidding the holding of feasts in chapels built to the memory of Christian martyrs. Family fights in public had become a form of public entertainment—anticipating by some fifteen hundred years the television programs that rely on family conflict to amuse audiences. These Augustine quickly abolished.

In 395 Augustine was consecrated as a bishop and took over still more of the ailing Valerius's duties. When Valerius died not long after, Augustine became bishop of Hippo. Augustine established his household along quasi-monastic lines, simplicity being the rule. He also established the custom of once each year giving clothing to the poor in all the parishes of Hippo. He often put himself and his parishes into debt in order to help the poor. "I do not wish to be saved without you," Augustine said to the people of Hippo. "What shall I desire? What shall I say? Why am I a bishop? Why am I in the world? Only to live in Jesus Christ: but to live in Him with you. This is my passion, my honor, my glory, my joy and my riches."[62]

Augustine gained a reputation for inviting non-Christians to dine with him, and he was known for his affectionate and friendly nature. Often, however, he refused to eat with Christians whose conduct was causing a public scandal. He was strict about subjecting such people to penances and to the censure of the church. He complained that some sins had become so common that, while he personally condemned them, he did not want to oppose them too strongly in public for fear of doing more harm than good.

Many of Augustine's letters survive. In a letter to Jerome, probably the greatest Scripture scholar of the early church—who would later become St. Jerome—Augustine wrote, "I entreat you again and again to correct me confidently when you perceive me to stand in need of it; for though the office of a bishop be greater than that of a priest, yet in many things Augustine is inferior to Jerome."[63]

Augustine served as bishop of Hippo for thirty-five years, and he spent much of his energy opposing heresies of

THE FIVE MOST POPULAR SAINTS

one kind or another. One group, the Donatists, who thought themselves more spiritual and pure than other Christians, actually preached publicly that to kill Augustine would be a virtuous act. For Augustine, on the contrary, the church was "the homeland of sinners, the weak and the cowardly, as long as they found themselves in the condition of pilgrims. 'We don't leave the threshing floor of the Lord on account of the chaff,' he objected to the self-confident dividing of the world into the just and the reprobates. 'We do not break up the Lord's flock because of the goats, which are to be separated out only at the end.'"[64]

When Pelagius, a British monk, and his followers declared that one's eternal destiny depended upon one's own efforts and that divine grace was of no help, Augustine preached against such errors without personally attacking Pelagius. At the same time, Augustine's theology had its unbalanced aspects. He believed, for example, that women were suitable only for "help in begetting children."[65] He also taught that original sin was passed down through the human race biologically, by sexual intercourse. Therefore, the only justification for sex, even in marriage, was for the sole intention of conceiving a child. Any other intention was sinful. Eluding black-and-white distinctions, however, Augustine did take some steps toward understanding the equality of men and women. He wrote that in marriage "both partners should be aware of their dignity."[66] In his final book, the monumental *City of God*, Augustine praised "the wonderful power of sex."[67]

In May 430 the Vandals laid siege to Hippo and would continue their attack for the next fourteen months. After three months, Augustine contracted a fever that would be the end of him. He knew he was on death's doorstep, and he declared often, "We have a merciful God." As he lay in his bed, Augustine asked that the penitential psalms be written out on tablets and hung on the wall where he could see them. He read these psalms as he lay there, tears in his eyes. Gradually, Augustine declined, and on August 28, 430, he died. He was seventy-six years old, and he died having just spoken the words of the pagan philosopher Plotinus: "There is no greatness in anyone who considers it very important when trees and stones fall and humans, who have to die, actually do die."[68]

St. Augustine's feast day is August 28.

St. Mary

The central figure in Christianity is Jesus of Nazareth, who is Lord and Messiah. Jesus is the Son of God, fully human and fully divine, and it is through his life, death, and resurrection that we gain salvation, that is, spiritual healing and liberation, for both this life and the next. Since the time of the early Christian community, however, believers have held another figure in a place of honor second only to Jesus. That figure is Mary, the mother of Jesus.

It was through Mary and through her "yes" to God that Jesus came into the world. The Gospel of Luke's account is more theological than historical, but the theological content of what Mary did is what matters:

> In the sixth month the angel Gabriel was sent by God
> to a town in Galilee called Nazareth, to a virgin engaged

to a man whose name was Joseph, of the house of David. The virgin's name was Mary. And he came to her and said, "Greetings, favored one! The Lord is with you." But she was much perplexed by his words and pondered what sort of greeting this might be.

The angel said to her, "Do not be afraid, Mary, for you have found favor with God. And now, you will conceive in your womb and bear a son, and you will name him Jesus. He will be great, and will be called the Son of the Most High, and the Lord God will give to him the throne of his ancestor David. He will reign over the house of Jacob forever, and of his kingdom there will be no end."

Mary said to the angel, "How can this be, since I am a virgin?" The angel said to her, "The Holy Spirit will come upon you, and the power of the Most High will overshadow you; therefore the child to be born will be holy; he will be called Son of God. And now, your relative Elizabeth in her old age has also conceived a son; and this is the sixth month for her who was said to be barren. For nothing will be impossible with God."

Then Mary said, "Here am I, the servant of the Lord; let it be with me according to your word." Then the angel departed from her. (1:26–38)

Mary is like all the saints, but her role is obviously unique, and far more attention has been given to her over the centuries than to any "ordinary" saint. Because she is the mother of the Son of God, she has been the subject of considerable theological reflection—even doctrinal development—and devotion to her takes many forms in various times, places, and cultures. In the words of the esteemed Lutheran historian Jaroslav Pelikan, "Concerning no other merely human being, none of the prophets or apostles or saints, has there been even a small fraction of the profound theological reflection that has been called forth by the person of the Blessed Virgin Mary."[1]

There is more to be said about Mary, in other words, than to simply tell the story of her life. Indeed, Mary "is not exclusively Catholic or Jewish, Western or Eastern, but a sign of what men and women can be when they participate in the ongoing mystery that links the divine to all that is."[2]

Unlike her son, Mary has no divine nature; she is a human being pure and simple. As the names of countless churches, schools, hospitals, and other institutions attest, she is first of all "St. Mary." We might say that Mary is the number one saint, and devotion to her among Christians down to our own time supports this statement. No other saint in the two millennia of Christian history even comes close to Mary in terms of popularity, and no other saint has a grip on the Christian imagination comparable to hers.

But who is Mary, and why does she evoke such intense feelings and so much popular devotion? "The typical reminders we get of her role as mother of Jesus can be misleading—pictures in museums and on Christmas cards can leave us with the impression that she was a woman of the Italian Renaissance. Our memories may be full of vague details that attach themselves to what we think we know about Mary, but that simply are not true."[3]

New Testament Passages about Mary

If we look for the real, historical Mary in the New Testament, we won't have much luck. We can be sure of little more, historically, than that she was a Jewish girl about age sixteen, living in a land occupied by a foreign military force, the Romans, and that she gave birth to Jesus between 7 and 4 B.C. (a quirk of the calendar caused by a later miscalculation). Apart from this, what we have in the Gospels are four unique presentations of Mary and her theological meaning and role, plus a passage in the book of Revelation about "a woman clothed with the sun" (12:1), often mistakenly interpreted as referring to Mary.

The only mention of Mary in Mark's Gospel—the earliest of the four—actually portrays Mary in a rather negative way. When Mary and "his brothers" (3:31) show up where Jesus is teaching and send word that they want to see him, Jesus replies in what seems to us an insensitive manner. Without responding to his mother's request, he uses the situation to make a theological point that may be interpreted as locating "his mother and his brothers" outside the circle of those who constitute his real family based on faith:

> And he replied, "Who are my mother and my brothers?"
> And looking at those who sat around him, he said,
> "Here are my mother and my brothers! Whoever does
> the will of God is my brother and sister and mother."
> (3:33–35)

The Gospel of Matthew's infancy narrative tells us only that Mary fulfilled the ancient promise of Isaiah that a virgin would conceive and give birth to a son who would be called Emmanuel, Hebrew for "God with us." Matthew says that Joseph, Mary's husband, receives the news about this event, but Mary is the one who is pregnant by the Holy Spirit:

> An angel of the Lord appeared to him in a dream and
> said, "Joseph, son of David, do not be afraid to take
> Mary as your wife, for the child conceived in her is
> from the Holy Spirit. She will bear a son, and you are
> to name him Jesus, for he will save his people from
> their sins." All this took place to fulfill what had been
> spoken by the Lord through the prophet: "Look, the
> virgin shall conceive and bear a son, and they shall
> name him Emmanuel," which means, "God is with us."
> (1:20–23)

In Luke's Gospel, on the contrary, we find a thoroughly positive portrait of Mary. Even in the scene in which Mark's

ST. MARY

Gospel gave us a less-than-flattering perspective on Mary, Luke tones that down considerably. Now it is even possible to interpret Jesus' words as including Mary among those who hear the word of God and act on it:

> Then his mother and his brothers came to him, but they could not reach him because of the crowd. And he was told, "Your mother and your brothers are standing outside, wanting to see you." But he said to them, "My mother and my brothers are those who hear the word of God and do it." (8:19–21)

Luke's infancy narrative uses considerable literary skill to portray Mary in positive ways. Here we find the well-known encounter between Mary and the angel Gabriel, with Mary's positive response to the angel's announcement. Here we find the meeting between Mary and her cousin Elizabeth, and we read Mary's canticle, the *Magnificat,* in which she praises God for all he has done for her and for all who are poor and lowly. Here we find the account of Jesus' birth in a stable in Bethlehem because there is no room anyplace else. Here we find the story of the shepherds and their visit to the infant Jesus. Here we find the story of the presentation of Jesus in the temple, where Simeon tells Mary of her own future suffering.

Finally, Luke completes his portrait of Mary, in the Acts of the Apostles, by telling his readers that Mary was present with the disciples in Jerusalem after the ascension of Jesus.

There she prays with the others, awaiting the coming of the Holy Spirit. Thus Luke offers Mary as a model of faith and a member of the first Christian community:

> Then they returned to Jerusalem from the mount called Olivet, which is near Jerusalem, a sabbath day's journey away. When they had entered the city, they went to the room upstairs where they were staying, Peter, and John, and James, and Andrew, Philip and Thomas, Bartholomew and Matthew, James son of Alphaeus, and Simon the Zealot, and Judas son of James. All these were constantly devoting themselves to prayer, together with certain women, including Mary the mother of Jesus, as well as his brothers. (1:12–14)

One of the many ways that the Gospel of John is unique among the four is that it never uses Mary's name, always referring to her as "the mother of Jesus." All the same, she appears in two important situations. The Fourth Gospel offers a theologically developed understanding of Mary that goes beyond what we find in the first three Gospels.

First, the wedding feast at Cana (John 2:1–11) occurs at the beginning of Jesus' public ministry. Here Mary is instrumental in the first of Jesus' signs (John never uses the word *miracle*). Mary brings to Jesus' attention that there is no more wine and instructs the servants to do what Jesus tells them to do. Jesus first protests, "Woman, what concern is that to you and to me? My hour has not yet come" (2:4). But then, at his mother's request, he helps the newly wed couple by turning water into high-quality wine.

Clearly, John understands that there is a significant relationship between Jesus and his mother. Throughout John's Gospel, in a very real sense, Jesus is already the risen Christ. For John to portray the mother of Jesus influencing her—in a certain sense already risen—son's actions clearly suggests that the Johannine community had an active devotion to Mary and a certain understanding of her relationship with the risen Christ, even as the Gospel took shape in the late first century.

Second, at the end of the Fourth Gospel, the mother of Jesus, Mary Magdalene, some other women, and the disciple whom Jesus loved remain near the cross as Jesus dies. "When Jesus saw his mother and the disciple whom he loved standing beside her, he said to his mother, 'Woman, here is your son.' Then he said to the disciple, 'Here is your mother.' And from that hour the disciple took her into his own home" (19:26–27).

Here the "beloved disciple" may well represent the new community of faith. This suggests the theological insight that in John's Gospel there is a significant relationship not only between Mary and the risen Christ but also between Mary and all of us, the church.

The final New Testament texts that apply to Mary were not written about her at all. Chapter 12 of the book of Revelation includes the following:

> A great portent appeared in heaven: a woman clothed with the sun, with the moon under her feet, and on her head a crown of twelve stars. She was pregnant and was crying out in birth pangs, in the agony of giving birth. Then another portent appeared in heaven: a great red dragon, with seven heads and ten horns, and seven diadems on his heads. His tail swept down a third of the stars of heaven and threw them to the earth. Then the dragon stood before the woman who was about to bear a child, so that he might devour her child as soon as it was born. And she gave birth to a son, a male child, who is to rule all the nations with a rod of iron. But her child was snatched away and taken to God and to his throne; and the woman fled into the wilderness, where she has a place prepared by God, so that there she can be nourished for one thousand two hundred sixty days. (12:1–6)

Scripture scholars tell us, "A traditional Roman Catholic interpretation has been that [the woman] is Mary, the mother of Jesus, who is also the new Eve. Other suggestions are that she is the heavenly Jerusalem, personified wisdom, or the church."[4]

It is highly unlikely that the human author of Revelation had any intention of referring to Mary, the mother of Jesus. It is more likely that the woman is a metaphor representing the people of God, the church. Still, later Christian generations found in the woman an apt image for Mary, who gave birth to Jesus, and because we are brothers and sisters of Jesus through baptism, she becomes our mother too. Many images of Mary depict her with a crescent moon under her feet and/or a crown of twelve stars on her head.

Development of Beliefs about Mary

The early fathers of the church said relatively little about Mary, but three Marian themes gradually developed.

1. Mary began to be seen as the new Eve, who by her obedience to God cancels out the disobedience of the first Eve in the Garden of Eden (see Genesis 3:1–6).

2. Mary's physical virginity—clearly witnessed to by the New Testament—is perpetual, both before and after the birth of Jesus. At the same time, Mary's physical virginity is important not so much in itself as for its theological meaning: that her child was no ordinary child.

3. Because Mary is the mother of the Word, the Second Person of the Trinity, she is, in the Greek of the early church, *Theotokos*, "God-bearer," or mother of God.

This last title for Mary is the result of a fifth-century theological dispute not about Mary but about Jesus:

> Nestorius, the patriarch of Constantinople, argued that since Christ had two distinct natures, human and divine, the latter indwelling the former, Mary could be called the Mother of Christ but not the Mother of God. Against this the Council of Ephesus (431) ruled that since there was only one divine person in Jesus Christ, it could truly be said that Mary was the Mother of God. Although the focus of this decision was on Christology, it gave a major impetus to Marian devotion.[5]

During the Middle Ages, the notion that Mary had a maternal influence over God gained in popularity. People began to think of Mary as being able to deflect the just anger of Christ and gain mercy for sinners. In fact, in the Eastern Orthodox churches, Christians had been thinking along these lines for some time. A story known as the Theophilus legend was popular among Eastern Christians.

> The legend recounts the story of Theophilus, deacon of the bishop of Cilicia, who at first is so humble he refuses the bishopric. But then the devil tempts him and he becomes ambitious. He signs an official contract in blood, giving over his soul to the devil at death;

after that, he quickly achieves honor, power, and glory. But he also begins to feel guilty. Increasingly desperate, he prays before a statue of Mary until he falls asleep. In a dream he sees Mary tear up the contract; when he awakes, pieces of real parchment lie scattered around him. He thanks Mary, confesses to the bishop, and dies in peace a few days later.[6]

The Theophilus legend was used widely as a catechetical tool, to instruct people in the faith. A French theologian named Fulbert of Chartres—best known as the one who began building the cathedral of Chartres—told the story as part of his sermon on September 8, the Feast of the Nativity of Mary. This story showed, Fulbert declared, "that the Mother of the Lord rules everywhere in great magnificence, that she can easily send the holy angels to minister to us and cancel the pacts of hell according to her good pleasure."[7]

That the Theophilus legend had a profound impact on the Christian imagination is further attested to by its retelling in stained glass—in the windows of the cathedral of Chartres, in two windows of the Notre Dame Cathedral in Paris, and in church windows at Laon, Beauvais, Troyes, and Le Mans.[8] This is how powerful a good story can be.

Also highly influential in spreading Marian devotion during these centuries were the countless monks who populated Europe and whose monasteries practically equaled in number the fast-food restaurants of today. The monks increased the number of Marian feast days and chanted an Office of the Virgin. By halfway through the tenth century, the story of Mary's *dormition*, or falling asleep/dying and arriving in heaven, was widespread. In the eleventh-century cathedral of Canterbury, England, Mary is portrayed with a crown and scepter, symbols that suggest she had an important role in redemption.

Mary began to be seen as gifted by God in special ways so that she was called the channel by which divine grace flows to earth. She was compared to the neck between the head, Christ, and his body, the church. Marian titles appeared such as "mediator with the Mediator" and "mother of mercy and refuge of sinners." Mary was thought to be especially approachable because of her maternal love. The beginnings of what would become the doctrines of Mary's immaculate conception, that she herself was without original sin from the moment of her conception, and of her assumption, that she was assumed into heaven, body and soul, at the end of her life on earth, emerged during these centuries as well.[9]

It became common for people to show their devotion to Mary by making pilgrimages, by venerating Marian images, and by putting on dramatic plays based on stories of Marian miracles and apparitions. Many Marian devotions and new prayers to Mary became popular during the Middle Ages, including the Hail Mary and the Rosary, which are still used by many Catholics today.

During the Protestant Reformation in the sixteenth century, it was common for the followers of the original reformers—such as Luther, Zwingli, and Calvin—to criticize the huge popularity of Marian devotion. The fathers of the Reformation themselves, however, were not so inclined. "While it is true that many of the radical leaders who followed the original reformers sought to eliminate the Mother of our Lord from their theology, and in many cases were successful in all but doing so, this does not represent the position of the early leaders."[10]

The Counter-Reformation Council of Trent (1545–63), inconsistent with its generally strong response to Protestant attacks, responded in a remarkably restrained manner. It merely said that it was good and helpful to ask for the prayers of the saints, and it invited bishops in their dioceses to correct people whose Marian devotion was out of line with orthodox practice. Responses following the council were not so subtle, however. Catholic artists went out of their way to portray all the beliefs Protestants scorned. "A fresco by Domenichino in the church of San Gennaro in Naples depicts the triumph of the Virgin over the Reformation; the lower part shows a young hero treading on Luther and Calvin alongside a woman praying the Rosary. In heaven above, the Virgin portrayed as the Immaculate Conception accepts the woman's prayer."[11]

Protestants had fits about the Rosary, of course, so Pope Pius V responded by giving this popular Marian devotion official recognition. He also established the Feast of the Rosary, saying that the Italian naval victory over the Turks at Lepanto, on October 7, 1571, was due to the Rosaries recited that day. St. Peter Canisius, a Jesuit who died in 1597, championed the Rosary and saw in a renewal of Marian devotion the best way to correct the damage done by the Reformation.[12]

During subsequent centuries, Marian devotion increased. Mary's immaculate conception and assumption into heaven were declared dogmas by papal decrees in 1854 and 1950. Understandably, Protestants protested each decree vigorously.

Customs, Apparitions, and Other Marian Phenomena

If anything, Marian apparitions have become more influential, not less. In modern times, apparitions of Mary were reported at La Salette, Lourdes, Fátima, and other places, and many pious books about Mary were published, including the widely popular *The Glories of Mary* by St. Alphonsus Liguori.

Papal encyclicals celebrated Mary and encouraged devotion to her, and customs developed such as wearing the *miraculous medal,* a small medal related to a Marian apparition, and the *scapular,* two little patches of cloth with devotional pictures on them connected by two strips of ribbon and worn over both shoulders, one patch in front, one in back. Years dedicated to Mary were popular, as were Marian congresses. New feasts of Mary were added to the calendar, including the Queenship of Mary, August 22.

One of the most significant Marian apparitions occurred on December 9, 1531. The story is that Mary appeared as a young Indian girl to a poor Indian named Juan Diego and left miraculously imprinted a portrait of herself on his *tilma,* or cloak. The earliest account of this apparition was given in the Aztec language.

> According to this testimony, a "little Indian woman" first appeared to Juan Diego in a village near Mexico City, as he walked at daybreak at the foot of the small hill called Tepeyac. First he heard many birds singing in concert from the top of the hill. Then he noticed a white, shining cloud, and around it a beautiful rainbow of colors coming from a bright light in the middle of the cloud. He heard a woman call his name, telling him to come closer. She spoke in his native Nahuatl tongue and told him that she wanted a church built on this hill where, she said, "I will hear your weeping and prayers to give you consolation and relief. I will show my loving favor and the compassion I have for the natives and for those who love and seek me."[13]

The "little Indian woman" described herself to Juan Diego as "the ever-Virgin Mary, Mother of the true God by whom all live," using the Aztec name *Tonantzin,* "Mother of the Gods." She instructed Juan Diego to ask the bishop to build the church, but the bishop ignored him. Again she told him to go, and again he was rejected. Juan Diego pleaded with the woman to send someone else, someone of noble birth who would be listened to, but the woman kindly insisted that this was a job that "was fitting" for him.[14]

On December 12, Juan Diego found Castilian roses growing on Tepeyac, cold and bare as it was. He collected the roses into his tilma, and on his way to the city he met the woman again. She rearranged the roses and told him to open his tilma for no one but the bishop. When Juan Diego did so, the bishop was astonished to find imprinted there the now-famous image of Our Lady of Guadalupe. This name seems to have come from the Spanish translation of Juan Diego's Aztec name for the "little Indian woman," Tlecuauhtlacupeuh —which roughly translated means "St. Mary who appeared on the rocky summit."[15]

The native people of Mexico were overwhelmed, convinced that Mary's attitude toward them was not that of their Spanish oppressors.

Another part of the legend says that Mary appeared to Juan Diego's uncle and cured him of a serious illness, and this time she called herself "Mary who drives away those who eat us."[16] The Indians were impressed that the Virgin appeared as one of them, and they began to call her the *morenita,* "little dark one." Our Lady of Guadalupe made it possible for the native people of Mexico to accept the religion of the Spanish and keep their self-respect at the same time.

The church the "little Indian woman" requested was built on Tepeyac, and the indigenous people felt liberated by their devotion to Our Lady of Guadalupe. Today, Mexican American women report that from Our Lady of Guadalupe they gain freedom and empowerment.[17] Devotion to her has spread to all of Latin America.

Further apparitions of Mary in modern times led to the emergence of other well-known Marian devotions. These include La Salette (1846) and Lourdes, in France (1858), Fátima, in Portugal (1917), and various others. In each of these cases, after rigorous investigations the apparitions received subsequent church validation as authentic. More recently, Marian apparitions were reported in Medjugorje, a village in the Catholic Croatian region of the former Yugoslavia (1981), and the apparitions allegedly have continued since then. As of the publication of this book, however, official church validation of the apparitions at Medjugorje was not forthcoming.

The Second Vatican Council's Teachings on Mary

In the mid-1960s, the Second Vatican Council decided to include its teaching on Mary in a major document on the church (Lumen Gentium) rather than in a separate document on Mary. This placed Marian theology smack in the mainstream of the church's reflections on what it means to be a disciple of Christ. In chapter 8 of this document, the council placed Mary in the company of the other saints but with a unique status.

The council taught that Mary is a "preeminent and altogether singular member of the Church" (n. 53). As the mother of Jesus, Mary lived her life as a "pilgrimage of faith" (n. 58). Mary is a member of the church who is a model and example of faith, love, and union with Christ. As a mediator, Mary does not detract from the sole mediation of her son but reveals his power because his mediation gives rise among ordinary humans "to manifold cooperation which is but a sharing in this unique source" (n. 62). The council added that we "do not hesitate to profess this subordinate role of Mary" (n. 62).

We do not worship or adore Mary, the council continued, but we show her reverence as the God-bearer. We, the church, look to Mary with hope, for she is the first of what we are destined to become.

Church Doctrines regarding Mary

There are four major Marian doctrines in the church. Two of these are from ancient times; the other two are of modern origin, though based on ancient traditions. From the early centuries of the church comes belief in Mary's virginity before, during, and after the birth of Jesus. From this same period comes the belief that because Jesus is fully human and fully divine, Mary is truly the mother of God. The belief that Mary was herself conceived without original sin—the immaculate conception—was declared an official dogma in the nineteenth century. The belief that she was taken directly into heaven, body and soul, at the end of her life—the assumption— became an official dogma in the early twentieth century.

In every celebration of the Eucharist, or Mass, Mary is remembered in the company of the apostles, martyrs, and all the saints. In the course of the liturgical year, Catholics also honor Mary in various liturgical contexts. There are, for example, the Solemnities of the Immaculate Conception (January 1) and of the Annunciation of the Lord (March 25); the Feasts of the Visitation (May 31) and of the Birth of Mary (September 8); and the Memorials of Our Lady of Guadalupe (December 12) and of Our Lady of the Rosary (October 7).

Catholics also cultivate devotion to Mary by means of prayers and devotional practices both private and communal. These include the Rosary, pilgrimages to the sites of Marian apparitions, such as Lourdes and Fátima, and the veneration of Marian icons. In 1974 Pope Paul VI published an apostolic exhortation on devotion to Mary, *Marialis Cultus.* In this document the pope said that when we honor Mary, we need to keep clearly in mind that Christ alone is our Savior and the one Mediator between God and humankind. We should keep uppermost in mind the working of the Holy Spirit in the gift of grace, or God's self-gift to us. We should also remember the teaching of Vatican II that Mary is a model of what the church, meaning all of us, is to become.

Paul VI reminded us that devotion to Mary should be heavily affected by familiarity with the Scriptures, and devotion to Mary should be kept well within the context of the church's liturgy. It is also important to not give other Christian churches a mistaken idea of what we believe about Mary.

A contemporary feminist critique of Mary and Marian devotions takes as its starting point the experiences of women themselves and the goal of promoting the full humanity of women in our time. Although there are other legitimate ways to do theology, this particular approach is having an impact on, among other things, the understanding of Mary among educated women in affluent Western countries. In the words of one feminist student of Mariology,

> a feminist theology of Mary is taking on a completely new form and is offering a very different image of her from the traditional, culturally conditioned images that do little to uplift women in search of full humanity. Precisely as a woman her story will undoubtedly resonate with those of other women through bonds of sisterhood. The self-possessed poor woman of the annunciation narrative (Luke 1:26–38) who finds favor with God and is willing to cooperate with God's plan of salvation is a model of courage for the marginalized women of today's world. She stands in solidarity with the poorest of the poor of society.[18]

Devotion to Mary has been a part of Christianity from its earliest days. Though largely rejected in the sixteenth century by the Protestant Reformation, this practice has been retained in Catholicism, in Eastern Orthodox churches, and to a lesser degree in Anglican/Episcopalian churches. Devotion to Mary as the preeminent saint will remain one of the treasures of Catholicism no matter what modifications the future may hold for our understanding of her.

Catholics in all times look to Mary as a model for the full humanity that is God's gift to us. Catholics will always pray in the familiar words adapted from the greeting of the angel in the Gospel of Luke: "Hail, Mary, full of grace, the Lord is with thee, blessed art thou among women, and blessed is the fruit of thy womb, Jesus."

CHAPTER FOUR

Thoroughly Modern Saints

Most of the saints lived hundreds of years ago, some more than fifteen hundred years ago. While their stories continue to inspire and their faith continues to stand as an example of what it means to be a follower of Christ, we naturally find saints closer to our own time particularly intriguing. The closer a saint is to our own era, the more we can know about him or her, and the more similar our two worlds are historically. Also, a saint who lived near us in time became a saint in social and cultural conditions closer to our own than did a saint who lived in the fifth, twelfth, or sixteenth century. As delightful as a St. Teresa of Ávila continues to be for us today, and as much as her writings continue to carry much wisdom that benefits us, she lived in sixteenth-century Spain, and there are a great many differences between her world and ours.

In this chapter, therefore, we will focus on two women and one man who are canonized saints of our own era. We will look in some detail at the lives of these modern saints. Each one is an individual who began life in the late nineteenth century, lived his or her faith in a heroic fashion, and died in the twentieth century.

St. Maximilian Kolbe

Perhaps the most dramatic story of any twentieth-century saint is that of **Maximilian Kolbe (1894–1941).** He was a Franciscan friar and priest who lived in Poland. During World War II, in the infamous Nazi death camp at Auschwitz, Kolbe volunteered to give his life for another man.

Kolbe was born at Zdunska Wola, near Lodz, Poland, on January 7, 1894, and baptized with the name Raymond. A famous story from Raymond Kolbe's childhood accounts for his lifelong devotion to Mary. After his death in 1941, Kolbe's mother told the story:

> I have always known that [my son] was going to die a martyr because of an extraordinary event in his childhood.
>
> . . . One time I didn't like something about him, and I said to him, "My little son, I don't know what's going to become of you!" After this I never thought about my remark, but I soon noticed that my child had

changed so much that he was unrecognizable. We had a little hidden altar [in the house] at which he was frequently hiding himself. In general his behavior seemed older than his years. He was always . . . serious, and praying with tears in his eyes. I got worried that perhaps he was ill, so I asked him, "What's wrong with you?" I insisted, "You have to tell Mama everything."

Trembling and with tears in his eyes, he told me, "When you said to me, 'What will become of you?' I prayed very hard to Our Lady to tell me what would become of me. And later in the church I prayed again. Then the Virgin Mother appeared to me holding in her hands two crowns, one white and one red. She looked at me with love, and she asked me if I would like to have them. The white meant that I would remain pure, and the red that I would be a martyr. I answered yes, I wanted them. Then the Virgin looked at me tenderly and disappeared."[1]

In 1907, at the age of thirteen, Raymond entered the Conventual Franciscan minor seminary in Lwów, where his teachers were impressed with his intellectual and imaginative gifts. Raymond was particularly good at mathematics and physics, and he thought seriously of becoming a military officer.

By the time he was sixteen, however, after a difficult decision-making process, Raymond chose to enter the Con-

THOROUGHLY MODERN SAINTS

ventual Franciscan order and become a priest. At this time he received his new name, Maximilian. The next year, in 1911, he took temporary religious vows of poverty, chastity, and obedience, and his superiors sent him to Kraków for further studies. There his intellectual gifts were once more recognized, and Maximilian soon found himself in Rome studying at the Gregorian University and the International Seraphic College. Studying both philosophy and theology, he earned doctorates in both.

"By all accounts, Maximilian Kolbe was an unpretentious, warm-hearted, and immensely human person who once said he wanted nothing more from life than to 'learn how to love without limits.'"[2] The young Franciscan thrived in Rome's cosmopolitan environment, and living there helped him to gain a wider perspective on the world. He saw how widespread and pervasive were both good and evil in the world. Evil in particular was not difficult to find as World War I raged in Europe and later as the storm gathered that would become World War II.

At this same time, Maximilian became deeply intrigued by the role of Mary in the history of salvation. "Was Mary simply the sweet and delightful mother who really had a secondary position as far as the happiness and eternal destiny of humanity was concerned?"[3]

Theological reflection on the Blessed Mother became a major interest in Maximilian's life, and returning to his earlier interest in things military, he began to think of himself as the knight of Mary, the Immaculate Mother. He was deeply impressed by Mary as Queen of the Universe. He wrote:

> This is the age of the Blessed Virgin; now begins the era of Mary Immaculate. Mary is the Mother, the real Mother, of each one of us . . . and the Queen of Society. We must practically recognize Mary's mission as Queen and Mother, then let her act fully, freely; she will then have unheard-of triumphs; she will conquer every enemy.[4]

Maximilian's devotion to Mary may seem exaggerated and sentimental today, in our era of a renewed emphasis on the role of Christ as the sole mediator between God and humankind. It is important to keep in mind, however, that Maximilian Kolbe lived in eastern Europe during a historical period before the Second Vatican Council, a time when many people felt distant from Christ and needed a figure to help them feel closer to God. While there is nothing unorthodox about Maximilian Kolbe's devotion to Mary, we need to allow for the unique historical, cultural, and theological context in which he lived. Perhaps our own era could use more devotion to Mary than we typically have.

Before he was ordained a priest in April 1918, Maximilian asked his superiors if he could form a group of his fellow Franciscans into a sort of club he called The Knights of Mary

Immaculate. The purpose of the group was to further devotion to Mary, and the first meeting was October 16, 1917, one year before the end of World War I.

Young Father Kolbe returned to Poland, where he was assigned to teach church history and philosophy at the Franciscan seminary in Kraków. About the same time, the young priest began publishing a magazine he called *The Knight of the Immaculata,* a free magazine designed to communicate news about the church and its teachings. The magazine was an immediate success, so popular that in 1927 Father Kolbe and his fellow Franciscans built a large friary and printing plant near Warsaw on land donated for this purpose by a wealthy benefactor. Kolbe named this place *Niepokalanow,* "the City of Mary."

By 1938 Niepokalanow was the largest Franciscan community in the world. Some eight hundred friars dwelled there and produced eleven different publications. The *Knight* alone had a circulation of more than one million. Later, one of the friars who lived in Niepokalanow recalled, "The place was going almost twenty-four hours a day. . . . Father Kolbe was a very progressive man. He said, 'If Jesus or Saint Francis were alive now, they'd use modern technology to reach the people.' So before World War II, Niepokalanow had a radio station, was preparing for television, had the daily paper, and so on. He said, 'The more you know, the better you can serve God.'"5

On September 1, 1939, the Nazis invaded Poland, and Niepokalanow was in the direct flight path of Nazi bombers. Father Kolbe directed most of the friars to leave for their own safety, but he remained behind with a few helpers to direct the opening of the friary to refugees, as many as three thousand a day. "Father Kolbe ensured that they were fed, clothed, given medical care, and if necessary, spiritual counseling. It is said that he displayed an especially tender love for Jews and never turned a needy refugee away."[6]

On February 17, 1941, the Nazis arrested Father Kolbe, charged him with treason, and immediately shipped him to Pawiak prison. The following May, the Nazis sent him to their death camp at Auschwitz. A man named Sigmund Gorson was thirteen years old at the time and a fellow prisoner of Father Kolbe in Auschwitz. He recalled:

> I was always looking for some link to my murdered parents, trying to find a friend of my father's, a neighbor—someone in that mass of humanity who had known them so I would not feel so alone.
>
> And that is how Kolbe found me wandering around, so to speak, looking for someone to connect with. He was like an angel to me. Like a mother hen, he took me in his arms. He used to wipe away my tears. I believe in God more since that time. Because of the deaths of my parents I had been asking, Where is God? and had lost faith. Kolbe gave me that faith back.[7]

In August 1941, Father Maximilian Kolbe stood with his fellow prisoners in the prison yard of Auschwitz. A prisoner had escaped from cellblock 14, and SS commandant Rudolf Höss directed Deputy Commander Fritsch to select, in reprisal, ten prisoners to die by starvation. If another prisoner escaped, twenty would be selected for the same fate.

As Fritsch finished picking out the ten men who would die, one of them began to sob. "My wife and my children!" he cried. The man was Francis Gajowniczek, a forty-year-old sergeant in the Polish army. As Gajowniczek continued crying, Father Kolbe stepped forward from the rear ranks. "Herr Kommandant," he said, "I wish to make a request, please."

"What do you want?"

"I want to die in place of this prisoner," Father Kolbe said, gesturing toward Gajowniczek. "I have no wife or children. Besides, I'm old and not good for anything. He's in better condition." The priest knew how to play on Fritsch's Nazi prejudices against the weak, the infirm, the elderly.

"Who are you?" the commandant barked.

"A Catholic priest," Father Kolbe replied.

"Request granted," Fritsch said in a cruel tone of voice.

Father Maximilian Kolbe nodded as Francis Gajowniczek stepped back to his place.

On August 14, 1941, after two weeks in the starvation bunker, Father Kolbe was still alive. Impatient, the Nazis killed him with an injection of carbolic acid. The next morning, on the Feast of the Assumption of Mary, his body was taken to the Auschwitz ovens and burned.

A survivor of Auschwitz, George Bilecki, said:

> It was an enormous shock to the whole camp. We became aware that someone among us in this spiritual dark night of the soul was raising the standard of love on high. Someone unknown, like everyone else, tortured and bereft of name and social standing, went to a horrible death for the sake of someone not even related to him. Therefore it is not true, we cried, that humanity is cast down and trampled in the mud, overcome by oppressors, and overwhelmed by hopelessness. Thousands of prisoners were convinced the true world continued to exist and that our torturers would not be able to destroy it. More than one individual began to look within himself for this real world, found it, and shared it with his camp companion, strengthening both in this encounter with evil.[8]

On October 10, 1982, Pope John Paul II canonized Father Maximilian Kolbe a saint of the Roman Catholic Church. Present in St. Peter's Basilica in Rome was Francis Gajowniczek, the man with whom Father Kolbe traded places in Auschwitz.

St. Frances Xavier Cabrini

Born in a tiny Italian village on the Lombard plain, **Maria Francesca Cabrini (1850–1917)** was the youngest of thirteen children. Her parents were Augustine, a farmer, and Stella Oldini Cabrini. Maria Francesca was small and delicate as a girl. All the same, she was fascinated by stories of missionaries who traveled to foreign lands. She especially liked tales of adventure in the Orient, and she dreamed of becoming a missionary in China. By the time she was old enough to enter a religious community, however, none would accept her because she looked like such a weakling and her health was not strong.

By the time she was thirty, Frances had become a teacher. In 1874 Monsignor Serrati, the pastor of the parish, asked Frances if she would take over a small orphanage for girls called the House of Providence Orphanage, in the village of Codogno. The orphanage was something of a sore point because some years prior it was discovered that the woman who ran the orphanage was not taking good care of the girls; rather, they were ill fed and poorly clothed. Monsignor Serrati was not entirely open with Frances about conditions at the orphanage, however, fearing that if he told her how bad things really were, she would refuse to go there.

Frances arrived at the orphanage to find a crowd of frightened girls living in horrible conditions, and the crowning touch was a headmistress who had no intention of being cooperative. Startled by what she found, Frances nevertheless rolled up her sleeves and went to work. She wrote to her sister, asking for medical supplies and fabrics to make new clothes for the girls. Then she began to scrub and clean the large dormitory where the girls' beds were lined up against the walls. The antagonistic headmistress gave Frances nothing but grief, criticizing everything she did. Often Frances was reduced to tears, but she was determined not to give up. She organized classes for the girls, teaching them reading, math, and geography. She also shared her faith, teaching the girls that work is a way to love God.

For three years Frances worked at the House of Providence, and during that time she never gave up her dream of becoming a nun. Because she was so successful in her work at the orphanage, the bishop finally agreed to allow her and seven of the older orphaned girls to take vows of poverty, chastity, and obedience. The newly professed sisters continued their work at the House of Providence, and a few months later Frances discovered that the headmistress had been stealing money from the parish. She showed the bishop the evidence and demanded that he take action.

The bishop immediately closed the orphanage and suggested that Frances found a missionary order of nuns. Frances was stunned by the bishop's suggestion, but she agreed to look for a house. Frances and her little community of nuns moved into an abandoned friary at Codogno and founded

THOROUGHLY MODERN SAINTS

the Missionary Sisters of the Sacred Heart. Their mission would be to teach young girls. This was in 1880, and by 1887 the energetic Mother Cabrini had established a total of seven convents.

Mother Cabrini became famous throughout Italy, and she planned to send some of her sisters to China, but Pope Leo XIII advised her to send them to the United States instead. In 1889 Archbishop Corrigan of New York asked Mother Cabrini to work among the Italian immigrants who were pouring into the city almost daily. Later, after Mother Cabrini and her sisters arrived in America, the archbishop had to withdraw his invitation because he could not come up with proper facilities. All the same, Mother Cabrini saw the needs that were going unmet, and she decided to stay. "America is my ordained mission," she told the unhappy archbishop. "Excellence, in all humbleness, I must say, in America I stay."[9]

Even though she had an intense fear of the ocean, Mother Cabrini returned regularly to Italy to bring back more sisters. Eventually, too, she taught herself English as she and her sisters dedicated themselves to caring for the countless Italian immigrants arriving in New York City.

Conditions for the immigrants were terrible, and Mother Cabrini decided to establish an orphanage for the many children whose parents died from the foul conditions in the tenements they had to live in. Within a few months of her arrival in America, Mother Cabrini had established her orphanage, even in the face of opposition from powerful political forces and opposition from the archbishop himself. "Like Saint Teresa [of Ávila]," Mother Cabrini declared, "with five pennies and God, I can accomplish many great things."[10]

Mother Cabrini became an American citizen in 1909, and she had an amazing ability to get what she wanted when it came to the needs of others. Soon after she had established her orphanage in New York City, for example, she announced to her sisters that she wanted to move the orphanage to a beautiful 450-acre setting on the banks of the Hudson River, a rural setting that would help the children to grow up healthy and happy. A Jesuit community owned the property, but the Jesuits were willing to sell because they had been unable to dig a successful well.

Mother Cabrini, with hardly a penny in her pocket, told the Jesuits that she would buy their land. "The Jesuits are packing and going to another monastery they have built in Peekskill," she wrote. "I told them Our Lord is my banker and will not fail to help me find the money. These problems overcome my naturally weak condition and make me strong. The bigger the problem, the stronger I become. And now, I would like nothing better than a plate of rice Milanese and a glass of cool beer."[11]

On another occasion, Mother Cabrini had established an orphanage in Seattle. The year was 1912, and she received a message from the city saying that a new highway was to be built, and it would be going right through the spot where her orphanage was located. Mother Cabrini and a group of her sisters searched Seattle for a new location but were unsuccessful. That night, Mother Cabrini had a dream in which she saw a villa on a hill. The next day, she located the villa she had seen in her dream and said, "That paradise will be for our orphans, somehow or another."[12]

Returning to their convent, the nuns were exhausted from walking all day. Mother Cabrini did not want to pay for a taxi, however, so the nuns kept walking until suddenly a limousine came along with only one person inside. Mother Cabrini flagged down the limousine, and the woman passenger offered to give the nuns a ride home. As they rode along, Mother Cabrini told the woman of her dream and about the villa she had seen that day. Gradually, the woman realized that the villa Mother Cabrini described was her home and that her passenger was none other than the now-famous Mother Cabrini.

The woman explained that the villa belonged to her. She said that she had never thought of selling the grand home, but she would give it to Mother Cabrini if she would give her a glass of water. As soon as they arrived at the convent, Mother Cabrini gave the woman a glass of water, and Mother Cabrini turned the woman's home into an orphanage.

Mother Cabrini served as head of the community of nuns she had founded, caring for the poor, until her death on December 22, 1917. Mother Cabrini left behind more than fifty hospitals, schools, orphanages, convents, and other foundations. Following her death, those who had known Mother Cabrini began to pray, asking her to help them by her prayers. By the time she had been dead for ten years, some 150,000 reports of Mother Cabrini's intercession had been sent to the pope along with messages asking for her canonization. Finally, in 1950, Pope Pius XII canonized the little Italian woman as St. Frances Xavier Cabrini.

St. Edith Stein

Born into an Orthodox Jewish family in Germany, **Edith Stein (1891–1942)** had the gift of a sharp intellect and an independent spirit. When she was thirteen years old, she announced that she was an atheist. Accepted as one of the first women students at the University of Göttingen, Edith became the star student of the great philosopher Edmund Husserl, who made Edith his assistant at the University of Freiburg. Edith completed her doctoral dissertation under Husserl's direction, her topic being the nature of empathy.

Gradually, during the years after World War I, Edith Stein felt attracted to religion, and one night in 1921 at the home of a friend she came upon a copy of the autobiography of St. Teresa of Ávila. Totally engrossed, Edith stayed up all night to finish the book, and then she said, "This is the truth." On New Year's Day 1922, Edith Stein was baptized a Catholic.

Edith's Jewish relatives, particularly her mother, reacted with shock and sorrow when they learned of her conversion.

Still, there was nothing they could do, and Edith continued to go to the synagogue with her mother. She later said that by accepting Christ she felt that she had mysteriously rediscovered her Jewish origins.

For the next eight years, Edith taught in a Dominican girls' school, setting aside strictly academic studies and research. Yet her reading of the works of St. Thomas Aquinas kept alive her interest in academic studies. In 1932 she began teaching on the university level again, in Münster. When the Nazis came into power in Germany, however, Edith was soon dismissed from her position because she was Jewish.

Along the way, Edith had sensed a growing attraction to the religious life, and now that she had no teaching responsibilities, she decided to follow her heart. On April 15, 1934, Edith entered the Carmelite convent in Cologne and took the religious name Sister Teresa Benedicta of the Cross.

Four years later, on November 8, 1938, open persecution of Jews was declared in Germany. Not wanting to put the other sisters in her convent at risk, Edith surreptitiously escaped to a Carmelite convent in Holland. At the same time, Edith had no intention of escaping the fate of the Jewish people at the hands of the Nazis. Her intention, in fact, was to offer her own life for her people, for the prevention of war, and for her Carmelite community. Even this early, Edith foresaw what would happen. She later wrote:

I spoke with the Savior to tell him that I realized it was his Cross that was now being laid upon the Jewish people, that the few who understood this had the responsibility of carrying it in the name of all, and that I myself was willing to do this, if he would only show me how.[13]

The Nazis occupied Holland in 1940. Even though Edith belonged to a cloistered religious order, which meant she never went outside the convent, the Nazis required her to wear a yellow Star of David on her habit at all times. Edith's sister Rosa had also converted, and she came to the convent in Holland to be with Edith as a laywoman.

As long as the churches said nothing about the Nazi persecution and deportation of Jews, the Nazis said that Jewish Christians would not be harmed. In July 1942, however, the Catholic bishops of Holland publicly denounced the persecution of the Jews. Immediately, all Jewish Catholics, including those in convents or monasteries, were arrested. On August 2, the Gestapo took Edith and Rosa, and they were put on a train headed for a detention camp.

Witnesses later testified that Edith acted calmly and with courage at all times. She spent time in prayer, cared for frightened children, and offered comfort to women separated from their husbands and children. From the detention camp, Edith and Rosa were soon shipped off to Auschwitz. On August 9, 1942, they died in the gas chamber.

Edith Stein was beatified in 1987 by Pope John Paul II and canonized by the same pope in 1998. Both events caused controversy among Jews, who insisted that Edith died not for her Christian faith but because she was Jewish. While there is some validity to this complaint, it is also significant that Edith Stein understood her death to be in unity with her people, as a sacrificial act for the evil of her time, and with a clear identification with the cross of Christ.

CHAPTER FIVE

Legendary Saints and Legends about Real Saints

Most saints, and their stories, are firmly grounded in history. The church—meaning us—wants to offer as role models and sources of personal inspiration real people who lived real lives in the real world. That is what we need, after all: people who we know had the same joys and sorrows we have, for whom faith was just as much of a struggle as it is for us. The further we look back in history, however, the more likely we are to find saints who may or may not have actually existed and whose stories are more legend than fact. The stories of such "saints" leave history behind, but often in a most delightful—and sometimes helpful—way.

When we make the jump from historical information to legend, it is vitally important to remember that truth can be communicated in more ways than one. The discipline of literary criticism teaches us that many different literary styles communicate truth without necessarily communicating historical facts. Poetry and fiction can communicate truth without giving us historical information. There is much truth in T. S. Eliot's poem "The Waste Land," and the same goes for a novel such as *Silas Marner,* by George Eliot. You can even find truth in a comic strip, but it certainly isn't historical. Ditto for legends and tall tales, and some saints and stories about saints are as legendary as they can be.

While legendary saints probably are not historical, their stories can still nourish our spirituality and draw us closer to God and neighbor. At one end of the spectrum, the stories of some legendary saints carry profound theological insights. At the other end of the spectrum, other saintly legends are helpful because they encourage hilarity, and faith can always use more of that.

St. Christopher

Probably the most popular saint whose historical status is uncertain, **Christopher** apparently lived in Asia Minor—modern-day Turkey—during the third century and died about the year 250. Little is known about Christopher, and the historical value of what we do know is questionable. Matthew Bunson and others say that he was a martyr known originally as Kester.[1] According to tradition, Christopher was an ugly giant of a man who used his size to advantage. He made his living by carrying people across a river that had no bridge.

One day, according to the legend, a small boy asked to be carried to the other side. Christopher hefted the little boy onto his shoulder and walked into the river, but with each step the child grew heavier. Fearing for his own safety, Christopher struggled against the river's current. At this point, the boy revealed that he was the Christ child, and the reason he was so heavy was because he bore the weight of the world himself. Thus, *Christopher* means "Christ-bearer."

Relics said to be those of Christopher are kept in both Rome and Paris. Originally, Christopher was the patron saint of ferry workers. Then this role expanded to include travelers, and in the twentieth century those traveling by automobile. Medals of St. Christopher are especially popular, often worn on a chain around the neck, kept on key rings, or displayed in automobiles, airplanes, boats, and other vehicles. Christopher "is invoked against sudden death, accidents, plagues, and all mortal danger."[2]

But does it make sense to pray to a legend, a largely fictional personage? It doesn't seem to make sense to ask a fictional or largely fictional character to pray for you. Unless, that is, there is more in the stew than a legendary character. Maybe there is more to praying to St. Christopher than meets the eye.

Granted, St. Christopher probably never existed. But the story of St. Christopher most definitely exists and holds powerful sway over the popular imagination. We pray to even the most historical saints not because they have some power independent of the power of God but because we want their companionship and prayers as we turn to God our loving Father with our needs and concerns.

Perhaps when people pray to St. Christopher, essentially what they do is turn to God in the company of a delightful story that God appreciates at least as much as they do. They turn to God with a story about a big ugly man who made his living doing people a kindness and who was favored by a visit from the Christ child. To pray to St. Christopher is to say to God, "Here I am praying for a safe journey for those I love and for myself. And, by the way, Lord, here is this wonderful story, too, which is a prayer in itself. Amen."

Chances are, God swallows this story hook, line, and sinker.

St. Wilgefortis

In the hilarity department, one of the front-runners is **Wilgefortis,** a saint whose existence is so doubtful that we don't even know when she lived. Let's just say that she lives in the mists of legend, which is where she belongs. In various parts of Europe Wilgefortis is known as Liberata, Kummernis, Virgo-Fortis, Uncumber, Livrade, and various other names.

According to the story, Wilgefortis was a virgin martyred for her faith. The young woman's father, a pagan Portuguese king with nine daughters, wanted her to marry in spite of her vow of virginity. So that she might escape the unwanted marriage, Wilgefortis grew a beard and mustache, which put the kibosh on the marriage in short order. Daddy, however, was not amused. So angry was Wilgefortis's father that he had her crucified.

No one relates to Wilgefortis as real today, but early Christian art portrayed her as a young girl with an admirable beard, carrying a cross shaped like a T. If her story has more than entertainment value, it would be in the form of inspiration: Look at the extent to which Wilgefortis was willing to go to maintain the integrity of her faith and her vow. From her story we can find smiling inspiration to be faithful too.

St. Christina of Tyre

A subcategory of legendary saints is saints who suffered spectacularly gory martyrdoms. **Christina of Tyre** belongs in this category. We have no dates for her, but supposedly she was a teenage Roman girl who was imprisoned for being a Christian. Christina repudiated her mother when she tried to get Christina to offer sacrifices to the pagan gods so that her life would be spared.

When threats failed to change Christina's mind, she was tortured in terrible ways. A fire was lit under her, but it got out of control, and hundreds were burned to death. Christina's breasts were cut off, and milk flowed from them. Her tongue was cut out, but after that she spoke even more clearly than before. She picked up her tongue and threw it at the judge. When Christina's tongue hit the judge in the eye, he lost his sight in that eye. When Christina was thrown into the ocean, she encountered Christ, who baptized her, and the archangel Michael returned her to land. As the legend goes, Christina recovered from all these tortures, but finally she was killed by being shot through the heart with an arrow. Nobody is invincible.

While it is highly doubtful that St. Christina ever lived, one must admit that her story is spectacular. At one time Christians must have been impressed by the power of her faith and by the extent, up to a point, to which God was willing to rescue her from her persecutors. Even today, stories such as this one may belong in the category—for kids, especially—of stories you love to be grossed out by.

St. Lawrence

Lawrence of third-century Rome is one of the best examples of a historical saint whose story became more inspirational through the addition of legendary elements. He was one of seven deacons who served the church in Rome, and he had important responsibilities, including the distribution of alms to the poor. In 257 the Roman emperor Valerian issued edicts against Christians, and Pope St. Sixtus II was taken prisoner and executed the following year. Four days later, Lawrence, too, became a martyr for the faith. This is all we know for certain.

According to later legend, as Pope Sixtus was led to his death, Lawrence followed him in tears, saying, "Father, where are you going without your deacon?" The pope replied, "I do not leave you, my son. You shall follow me in three days."[3] Overjoyed that he would be called to God in so short a time, Lawrence immediately went to seek out the poor, the widows, and the orphans to give them all the money he had at his disposal. Lawrence also sold chalices made of precious metals used for the liturgy, and he included that money in what he gave to the poor.

When a Roman official heard what Lawrence was doing, he concluded that the Christians must have a sizable treasure stashed away someplace, so he sent for Lawrence and said to him, "You Christians often complain that we treat you with cruelty, but no tortures are here thought of. I only inquire mildly after what concerns you. I am informed that your priests offer in gold, that the sacred blood is received in silver cups, and that in your nocturnal sacrifices you have wax tapers fixed in golden candlesticks. Bring out these treasures; the emperor has need of them for the maintenance of his forces. But I am told that according to your doctrine you must render to Caesar the things that belong to him. I do not think that your God causes money to be coined; He brought none into the world with Him; He only brought words. Give us therefore the money, and be rich in words."[4]

Lawrence replied that the church was, indeed, rich; in fact, the emperor had nothing to compare with the church's wealth. Lawrence said that he would bring the official the church's wealth if he could have some time to get it all collected, and the official agreed. So Lawrence went all over the city looking for the poor who looked to the church for their support, and on the third day he took with him a large number of cripples, lepers, orphans, widows, and defenseless young women. He showed them to the official, explaining that they were the church's treasure.

The official was furious, imagining that he and the emperor were being mocked. Knowing that Lawrence desired martyrdom, he told Lawrence that he would die, but very slowly. He had a large grill-like instrument built, with hot coals burning under it, and on this he placed Lawrence, tied so that he could not move. His body roasted, little by little. Christian witnesses reported that as he burned, Lawrence's body gave off a beautiful light and a sweet smell. Lawrence did not feel the pain at all, however, because the fire of divine love was so powerful in him.

After he had been on the grill for a long time, according to the legend, Lawrence turned to the executioner and said with a smile, "Let my body be turned; one side is broiled enough." Then, after the executioner turned Lawrence, he said, "It is cooked enough, you may eat."[5] After he prayed for the conversion of Rome and the spread of faith in Christ through the whole world, Lawrence finally expired.

As the story goes, several Roman senators who watched Lawrence die were so touched by his faith and heroism that they immediately became Christians. These men carried Lawrence's body to the Via Tiburtina, where they gave him an honorable burial. Lawrence's death was also the death of idolatry in Rome, as idol worship began to decline from that time on.

St. Lawrence is a good example of a saint who was probably historical but whose legend far exceeds the probable historical facts. The story is a great one, all the same, and it serves to inspire those in later eras whose faith is challenged or who are persecuted for their faith.

Seven Sleepers of Ephesus

Another utterly fictional tale that makes an entertaining and inspirational narrative is the story of the **Seven Sleepers of Ephesus.** According to a medieval source, *The Golden Legend,* by Jacobus de Voragine,[6] seven Christian men—John, Maximian, Constantine, Mortian, Malchus, Serapion, and Denis—were sealed into a cave, a unique form of execution, near Ephesus during the persecution of Emperor Trajanus Decius in the middle of the third century. The seven men went to sleep, and more than two hundred years later, during the reign of the Christian emperor Theodosius II, a landowner unsealed the cave to make it a place for his herdsmen to sleep. The seven martyrs awoke—Rip van Winkle–like—thinking they had slept but one night. Malchus went into Ephesus to obtain bread, and he was amazed to see the sign of the cross everywhere. When he went to buy bread, the bakers were astounded when Malchus paid with coins almost three centuries old.

As the light began to dawn on Malchus, he became terrified to the point of speechlessness. The bakers took Malchus to the bishop, Martin, and the Roman consul, Antipater, but Malchus thought he was being taken to the emperor, Decius. When led into the presence of Martin and Antipater, Malchus explained his situation as best he could, and the bishop and consul were astonished at what they heard. Malchus then led them out of the city to the cave where he and his friends had slept for so long. "And they saw the saints sitting in the cave and their visages like unto roses flowering, and they, kneeling down, glorified God."[7]

Soon the emperor was sent for, and when he arrived the seven sleepers witnessed to him about the power of the Resurrection. "And when they had said all this they inclined their heads to the hearth and rendered their spirits at the command of our Lord Jesus Christ, and so died. Then the emperor arose and fell on them, weeping strongly, and embraced them and kissed them debonairly. And then he commanded to make precious sepulchres of gold and silver and to bury their bodies therein."[8]

That night, the seven sleepers appeared to the emperor in a dream and asked him to leave their bodies lying on the ground, as they had while sealed in the cave, until they should rise again at the end of time. So the emperor ordered that the place "should be adorned nobly and richly with precious stones."[9]

In all likelihood, the story of the Seven Sleepers of Ephesus is pure fiction. Various forms of the story exist in both the East and the West. In the Eastern churches, in fact, the sleepers are said to have been children. A Greek Orthodox collection of prayers includes a prayer to the Seven Sleepers invoking their aid against sleeplessness. They are also still included in the Roman Martyrology.

The legend of the Seven Sleepers of Ephesus is as close as the stories of saints get to sheer fairy tale. But like fairy tales, stories such as this one function on both a conscious and an unconscious level, spiritually. On a conscious level we can delight in the sheer imaginative playfulness of the narrative. On an unconscious level, we benefit from the story as an encouragement to our own faith—which is itself proof that more goes on in the world than what meets the eye. Such stories remind us that in the life of faith, wonders are sometimes to be expected at the most unexpected times.

St. Thomas Becket

Thomas Becket (1118–70) is most certainly a real person and historical figure. But he also has the distinction of being widely recognized—thanks to the poet and playwright T. S.

Eliot—as a literary figure. In this sense, Thomas Becket's story has passed over from history into literature; the result is that the story itself has been inflated to mythic proportions.

The basic historical facts of Becket's life are well known. Born in London, England, on December 21, 1118, Thomas was the son of Gilbert Becket, sheriff of London, and his wife, Matilda. Thomas was well educated, and in 1141 he entered the household of Theobold, archbishop of Canterbury, who placed his trust in Thomas and gave him important responsibilities. Thomas was ordained a deacon in 1154 and soon became archdeacon of Canterbury.

In 1155 Thomas became chancellor of England, appointed by King Henry II. Soon he was the most powerful man in England, after the king. At this time, Thomas was widely known for his wealth and his luxurious lifestyle. He went with Henry on a military expedition to Toulouse in 1159 and rode at the front of his own troops.

When Archbishop Theobold died in 1161, King Henry named Thomas the new archbishop of Canterbury, despite Thomas's vigorous objections. Obediently, Thomas Becket resigned as chancellor and was ordained a priest the day before his consecration as archbishop. Deeply affected by what had taken place, Thomas changed his whole way of life, embracing a life of great austerity.

Before long Thomas came into conflict with Henry over issues related to clerical and church rights. In 1164 Thomas refused to accept the Constitutions of Clarendon, which included a denial that clerics had the right to be tried in ecclesiastical courts and to appeal to Rome. Thomas was forced to flee England, so he went to France, where he asked the pope, Alexander III, for help. Alexander did not wish to offend Henry, however, so he was no help to Thomas.

Neither Thomas nor the king would budge an inch, so Pope Alexander suggested to Thomas that he enter the Trappist abbey at Pontigny, France. Thomas did so. Henry responded in 1166 with a threat to throw all Trappists from his kingdom, so Thomas moved to St. Columba Abbey near Sens, which was protected by King Louis VII of France. Finally, Louis was able to mediate a reconciliation between Thomas and Henry in 1170, and Thomas returned to England.

Soon, however, conflict again developed between the two men, and Thomas excommunicated the archbishop of York and all the other bishops who had cooperated when Henry crowned his son, an act that was a blatant violation of the rights of the archbishop of Canterbury. Thomas said that he would not lift the excommunication unless all the bishops and the king swore allegiance to the pope.

Henry had a tizzy fit about this and in a rage shouted publicly that he wished he were rid of this prelate, who was such a source of trouble for him. Although Henry probably did not mean this, four of his knights thought he was serious. So, on December 29, 1170, the four knights murdered Thomas Becket in his cathedral. All of Europe was shocked, and Thomas was immediately proclaimed a martyr. In 1173 Pope

Alexander declared Thomas a saint. The next year, Henry did public penance, and the shrine of St. Thomas Becket became one of the most popular pilgrimage sites in all of Europe.

T. S. Eliot's famous play, *Murder in the Cathedral,* first performed in the late 1940s, adds to Thomas Becket's stature by portraying him in ways that glorify his holiness and inflate his character and personality beyond that of the actual historical person. At the same time, Eliot's play builds on the historical Becket and real events in his life in ways that communicate an authentic spirit of Christian heroism.

T. S. Eliot does Thomas Becket a great service by portraying him not as a two-dimensional figure but as a man of complex personality and motives. Four Tempters try to direct Becket away from virtuous action, for example, and Becket responds to each. The final Tempter is the most devious, and to her Thomas responds with the famous words, "The last temptation is the greatest treason: / To do the right deed for the wrong reason."[10]

T. S. Eliot places on the lips of Thomas Becket a homily, given on Christmas morning in the year 1170. In this homily, Becket talks about the meaning of Christian martyrdom, a topic that takes on added poignancy since Becket himself will soon become a martyr:

> Beloved, we do not think of a martyr simply as a good
> Christian who has been killed because he is a Christian:
> for that would be solely to mourn. We do not think of

him simply as a good Christian who has been elevated to the company of the Saints: for that would be simply to rejoice: and neither our mourning nor our rejoicing is as the world's is. A Christian martyrdom is no accident. Saints are not made by accident. Still less is a Christian martyrdom the effect of a man's will to become a Saint, as a man by willing and contriving may become a ruler of men. Ambition fortifies the will of man to become a ruler over other men: it operates with deception, cajolery, and violence, it is the action of impurity upon impurity. Not so in Heaven. A martyr, a saint, is always made by the design of God, for His love of men, to warn them and to lead them, to bring them back to His ways. A martyrdom is never the design of man; for the true martyr is he who has become the instrument of God, who has lost his will in the will of God, not lost it but found it, for he has found freedom in submission to God.[11]

The Thomas Becket of Eliot's play is Becket become a legend, but in a way that remains true to the ideals and essence of who St. Thomas Becket was and is. T. S. Eliot gives us a character who reveals the deepest meaning of Thomas Becket. When the three priests try to save Thomas by getting him to come with them to vespers, he replies, "Go to vespers, remember me at your prayers. / They shall find the shepherd here; the flock shall be spared. / I have had a tremor of bliss, a wink of heaven, a whisper, / And I would no longer be denied; all things / Proceed to a joyful consummation."[12]

Later, as he dies, Thomas's words become more than merely his own words, but the words of anyone who has ever died for the faith: "Now to almighty God, to the Blessed Mary ever Virgin, to the blessed John the Baptist, the holy apostles Peter and Paul, to the blessed martyr Denys, and to all the Saints, I commend my cause and that of the Church."[13]

St. Thomas Becket, the historical figure, was like all saints an imperfect human being who, by God's grace, became, in spite of his imperfections, a sign of God's love in the world. The Thomas Becket of *Murder in the Cathedral* is the same man, but by means of literary license T. S. Eliot unpacks Becket and his martyrdom to show us meanings that would otherwise remain obscure.

CHAPTER SIX

Saints of Many Kinds

Not only are there legendary saints and legends about real saints, but among saints whose existence is clearly historical there is quite a variety. As we have already seen, there are martyrs, saints who died for the faith, and confessors, saints who gave witness to the faith in a very public manner. Following is a list of saint categories:

apologists: those who used their intellectual gifts to defend the faith

apostles: the twelve disciples Jesus chose to be with him during his earthly ministry, with the exception of St. Paul, who converted to Christianity and became an apostle after the resurrection of Jesus, and Matthias, chosen to replace Judas, who betrayed Jesus

bishops and popes: those who were called to serve the Lord as official leaders of the church

catechists: those who instructed people in the Christian faith

disciples of the Lord: those who were followers of Jesus during his earthly life

doctors of the church: those recognized for their theological wisdom

educators: those who (usually) built schools

exorcists: those who drove out evil spirits from possessed persons (an extremely rare phenomenon today)

hermits: those who lived a life of prayerful solitude

married men and women: those who lived saintly lives in the context of marriage and family (there are very few saints in this category)

missionaries: those who proclaimed the gospel in distant lands

presbyters and deacons: those who were ordained to the priesthood or diaconate

religious: those who belonged to religious orders

religious founders: those who established religious orders

virgins: those (women) who renounced the normal pleasures of life, in particular marriage and sex, for the sake of the gospel

In a few cases, some saints are the only ones of their kind. Sts. Joachim and Anne, for example, are listed as "parents of the Virgin Mary."

In many cases, saints belong to more than one category. This is why, if you look at a calendar with liturgical information on it, you will see entries such as—on July 15, for example—"Bonaventure, bishop, religious, doctor of the church." St. Clare of Assisi is "virgin" and "religious founder," while St. Bridget of Sweden is "married woman" and "religious founder." St. Charles Borromeo is, however, listed only as "bishop."

There are, indeed, saints who were married, such as St. Bridget of Sweden, St. Henry the Emperor, and St. Elizabeth Ann Seton. But as of the writing of this book, no couple has been recognized for becoming saintly *by being married.* There has been some talk of canonizing Louis and Zélie-Marie Martin, the parents of the nineteenth-century French saint Thérèse of Lisieux. Some ask, however, if the Martins would be considered holy for having a holy marriage or for being the parents of a saint. Most parents would be discouraged, not inspired, by a couple who produced a saint!

"What this typology suggests," wrote Kenneth L. Woodward, "is not that the church, in the process of making saints, is blind to the candidate's real-life vocation, but that the idea of sanctity continues to be identified at root with forms of renunciation as expressive of the love of Christ."[1]

It is important to note, Woodward continued, that even in the church's early centuries Christians saw more in the saints than their willingness to die for the faith and their heroic renunciation—both, to be sure, an imitation of Christ. The early Christians also saw the saints as instruments of Christ the wonder-worker. Saints, while alive in this world, sometimes cured people of various afflictions but never claimed any credit for themselves. Rather, it was always the power of Christ and his resurrection at work.[2]

Following the death of a saint, miracles sometimes occur through the saint's intercession—*through* prayer asking the saint to pray on someone's behalf—and these also are viewed as the power of Christ at work through the saint. Indeed, no one can be canonized a saint unless one such miracle is proven to have happened through the saint's intercession. But the point is that heroic holiness means more than various forms of renunciation; it also means becoming an instrument of Christ in the world. This is important for ordinary Christians to understand, since this form of holiness is accessible to everyone.

We will now take a brief look at a particularly prominent saint in several of the categories already mentioned. This will give you a better idea of what each of these categories means in the lives of saints who were real human beings who lived in the real world.

St. Francis Xavier: Missionary

One of the greatest missionary saints of all time is **Francis Xavier (1506–52).** Francis was born on April 7 in his family's castle near Pamplona, in the Basque region of Spain. While studying at the University of Paris, he met the future saint Ignatius of Loyola, who was cooking up plans to found the Jesuit order. At first, Francis opposed Ignatius's ideas, but eventually he agreed and became one of the first seven Jesuits who took their vows in 1534.

Francis was ordained a priest in 1537 along with Ignatius and four others. He traveled to Rome in 1538, and two years later—the year the Society of Jesus received papal approval—he and Father Simon Rodriguez became the first Jesuit missionaries when they were sent to the East Indies.

Francis and Simon stopped over in Lisbon, Portugal, where they were detained by King John III, who insisted that Simon remain. After eight months, Francis finally continued to the Orient on April 7, 1541. He reached Goa thirteen months later and spent the next five months preaching, caring for the sick and those in prison, teaching classes for children, and trying to reform the ways of the Portuguese population. Francis especially preached against concubinage, or "shacking up." Today this practice goes by the nonjudgmental sociological term *cohabitation.*

At any rate, concubinage was widespread in Portugal at the time, and Francis Xavier let it be known in no uncertain terms that "living together" was not in accord with God's will. Francis was ahead of his time, it would seem, as recent studies indicate that couples who live together before marriage have a much higher divorce rate than couples who don't cohabit before they marry.[3]

Francis then spent three years at Cape Comorin, located at the southern tip of India, where he baptized thousands of people. In 1545 he visited Malacca and the Moluccas (near New Guinea), and 1546–47 found him in Morotai (near the Philippines) and Japan. Francis landed at Kagoshima in 1549, learned to speak Japanese, and set out for Kyoto, which was then the capital of Japan. Two years later, Francis left Japan in the care of another Jesuit and returned to Goa. In 1551 Ignatius established India and the East as a separate Jesuit province, and Francis became the first provincial superior.

In 1552 Francis Xavier departed for China, which he had always dreamed of evangelizing, but he died on the island of Sancian, just off the coast of China, near Canton. Francis caught a fever, and he died on December 3 while waiting for permission to enter China. His body was returned to Goa, where he was buried in the Jesuit church there. We can only speculate as to how different history might have been had Francis brought the message of the gospel to the Chinese. He was canonized a saint in 1662.

St. Francis Xavier traveled many thousands of miles under dangerous conditions, and he converted many thousands of people to Christianity. "Working with inadequate funds," wrote John Delaney, "little co-operation, and often actively opposed, he lived as the natives and won them to Christianity by the fervor of his preaching, the example of his life, and his concern for them."[4]

St. Clare of Assisi: Religious Founder

Best known as the friend and confidant of St. Francis of Assisi, **Clare (1194–1253)** founded the women's contemplative order known today as the Poor Clares. She was born into an affluent family, and when she was twelve she refused to marry. During Lent of the year 1212, Clare was so impressed by a sermon given by Francis that she ran away from home on Palm Sunday and received the Franciscan habit from Francis.

Because there was no convent for Franciscan women, Clare lived with a group of Benedictine nuns at the convent of St. Paul, near Bastia. When her family tried to forcibly remove her and take her home, Clare resisted. Soon after this, Francis helped Clare move to Sant' Angelo di Panzo convent, and her sister Agnes joined her.

Clare's father sent twelve armed men to bring Agnes back, but to no avail. According to what is probably a delightful pious legend, Clare prayed up a miracle, and Agnes became so heavy the men couldn't budge her, so they gave up and went away.

Clare moved to a house attached to the church of San Damiano in 1215, and Francis appointed her superior of the

SAINTS OF MANY KINDS

community. Thus the Poor Clares were founded. Clare and Agnes were joined by their mother, their sister Beatrice, and three women from the prominent Ubaldini family from Florence. Other women soon arrived. The little community of Poor Clares lived according to a strict rule and embraced absolute poverty.

In the course of her lifetime Clare's prayers led to many miracles. In 1241 the citizens of Assisi believed that Clare's prayers saved the town from attack by the soldiers of Emperor Frederick II. After Francis, Clare gets the most credit for the growth and widespread popularity of the Franciscans. She died in 1253, some twenty-seven years after Francis, and she was canonized a saint two years later.

St. Catherine of Siena: Doctor of the Church

Born in Siena, Italy, **Catherine Benincasa (1347–80)** was the youngest of twenty-five children. When she was only six years old, she began to have the mystical experiences that would occur throughout her life. Keep in mind that, from a Christian perspective, *mystical experiences* refers to a deeply felt love for God and neighbor. Sometimes, as in Catherine's case, mystical experiences include extraordinary phenomena, but all true mystics dismiss such phenomena as unimportant, even as distractions from what matters most, the love of God and neighbor.

Catherine's parents wanted her to marry, but she wanted nothing to do with marriage, preferring to give herself to prayer and fasting. When she was sixteen, Catherine became a tertiary, or lay member, of the Dominican order after she began to have visions of Christ, Mary, and the saints, which alternated with visions of evil and periods of spiritual dryness.

More important—and a more reliable sign of Catherine's mysticism than her visions—she spent much of her time caring for people in hospitals. She devoted herself to caring for patients with especially terrible diseases such as leprosy and terminal conditions we would today call cancer. At the same time, Catherine's mystical experiences attracted both supporters and detractors. The many who thought she was a phony used their influence to have her brought before a general chapter of the Dominicans in Florence. But the members of the general chapter dismissed the charges.

Returning to Siena, Catherine dedicated herself to caring for victims of a plague that killed thousands as it swept the city. She also cared for prisoners condemned to death. Catherine was widely recognized for her holiness, her ability to help those who were spiritually troubled, and her gifts as a peacemaker.

In 1375 Catherine visited Pisa and her presence in that city brought about a religious revival. While in Pisa she received the stigmata—the wounds of Christ in hands, feet, and side—but only after her death was this sign visible to others.

SAINTS OF MANY KINDS

Catherine wrote letters to Pope Gregory XI, taking him to task for doing nothing about the widespread corruption among the clergy and bishops:

> Don't be a fearful baby, be a man. God orders you to deal strictly with the excess of depravity of all those who gorge themselves in the garden of the holy Church. Rip out the evil smelling flowers, I mean the bad shepherds and administrators who are poisoning this garden. Bishops should seek God instead of living like pigs.[5]

Catherine also urged the pope to return the exiled papacy from Avignon, France, to Rome. In 1376 Pope Gregory finally did as Catherine wanted.

Returning to Siena, Catherine spent much of her time writing accounts of her mystical experiences. When Gregory XI died in 1378, the new pope, Urban VI, turned out to be a surprise to the cardinals who had elected him, and he so alienated them that they decided to elect a different pope. This breach was the beginning of what became known as the Great Western Schism, in which first two, then three popes existed at the same time.

Catherine was emotionally devastated by this division in the church. She worked tirelessly to gain support for Urban, but at the same time she did not hesitate to criticize him for some of his actions. To his credit Urban VI received Catherine's criticisms with equanimity and brought her to Rome, where she continued her efforts to reunite the church.

While in Rome, Catherine suffered a cerebral hemorrhage, and even though she was suffering from it, every morning she walked more than a mile to the grave of St. Peter to pray, "to work a little in the boat of the holy Church," as she said.[6] Catherine finally died on April 29. She was thirty-three years old, and she left hundreds of letters to people in every class of society, plus her *Dialogues,* the account of her mystical experiences. Catherine was canonized a saint in 1461, and she was named a doctor of the church in 1970.

St. Charles Lwanga: Catechist

In the mid-1880s, in Uganda, **Charles Lwanga (d. 1886)** was a master of pages at the court of a tribal chieftain, Mwanga. Charles succeeded Joseph Mkasa, a Catholic who had criticized Mwanga for forcing young page boys to have sex with him. Mkasa also called Mwanga to task for the murder of a Protestant missionary. Mwanga had Joseph Mkasa beheaded for his trouble.

Charles Lwanga was also a Catholic, and he baptized several of the pages and saved some of them from the lust of Mwanga. Furious, Mwanga called the pages together and ordered the Christians to separate themselves from the rest. Fifteen boys, some as young as thirteen, stepped forward, and

SAINTS OF MANY KINDS

Mwanga asked them if they planned to remain Christians. The boys shouted, "Till death!"[7]

Mwanga commanded that Charles Lwanga and the fifteen page boys be taken to a place called Namugango, thirty-seven miles away, and executed. Three of the boys were killed along the way, and when the group reached Namugango, the executioners built a fire, wrapped Charles and the pages in reed mats, and threw them on the pyre. "They all died calling on the name of Jesus."[8]

As so often happens, the example of Charles Lwanga and the young pages only served to promote the cause of the gospel. Mwanga launched a systematic slaughter of all Christians in the area, including several Protestant missionaries, but within a year hundreds of people were baptized. Twenty-two people were canonized in 1964 by Pope Paul VI as the Martyrs of Uganda. Because he was clearly instrumental in teaching the gospel to many of those who died—indeed, he was executed for doing so—Charles Lwanga was singled out for special honor.

St. Maria Goretti: Virgin

Many female saints are in the category of "virgin" simply because they were nuns. **Maria Goretti (1890–1902),** however, was not a nun, and she became a saint because she refused forcible sexual advances. As Kenneth L. Woodward pointed out, Maria Goretti did not, strictly speaking, die for her faith. Rather, she died "in defense of Christian virtue."[9] As we shall see, St. Maria Goretti remains the focus of debate even today.

Maria Goretti was born at Corinaldo, near Ancona, Italy, the daughter of Luigi Goretti, a farmworker, and Assunta Carlini. Later the family moved to Ferrier di Conca, near Anzio, in Italy's Potine marshes. When Maria was six years old, her father died from malaria, forcing her mother to support Maria and her six siblings. While her mother and brothers and sisters worked in the fields, Maria stayed home to take care of the house and prepare meals—a considerable task for a family of eight.

In July 1902 Maria, not quite twelve years old, sat at the top of the stairs mending a shirt. Alessandro Serenelli, the nineteen-year-old son of her father's partner in tenant farming and a boy Maria had known her whole life, entered the house. He tried to force himself on Maria. Alessandro had tried this before, but Maria had always angrily refused. This time, however, the young man grabbed Maria, pushed her into a bedroom, and closed the door.[10]

Maria continued to resist and called for help. According to later testimony by her attacker, she said, "No, it's a sin! God does not want it!"[11] Alessandro was choking her, however, and no one heard her cries. Alessandro tore Maria's dress from her body, stabbed her eighteen times with a long knife, then ran out of the house.[12]

Maria was discovered in time to get her to the hospital in a horse-drawn cart, but attempts to save her life failed. As she lay in her hospital bed, Maria said that she forgave Alessandro and hoped to see him in heaven. She said that she had been afraid of him for many months but had been afraid to say anything because she thought it would cause trouble for her family.

Maria Goretti died after twenty-four hours, her mother at her bedside as well as the parish priest, who brought her communion. Alessandro was caught and sentenced to thirty years in prison. For most of that time he refused to repent of his crime, but then one night in a dream Maria appeared to him, gathering flowers and offering them to him. In the dream, Maria told Alessandro that she would pray for him. As a result, Alessandro Serenelli had a change of heart and repented of his crime, and after twenty-seven years in prison, he was released. The first thing he did was to visit Maria Goretti's mother and beg her forgiveness.

Meanwhile, Maria's story captured the imagination of the Italian people, and thousands prayed to her, asking her to pray for them. Hundreds of miracles were reported. Soon Maria Goretti became an international symbol of sexual purity. Pope Pius XII beatified Maria in 1947, appearing on the balcony of St. Peter's Basilica with her mother and two of her brothers. On this same occasion, the pope delivered an address in which he verbally chastised those in "the movie industry, the fashion industry, the press, the theater, and even

SAINTS OF MANY KINDS

the military, which had recently conscripted women, for corrupting the chastity of youth."[13]

In 1950 the same pope canonized Maria Goretti a saint. Present was the largest crowd ever to gather for a canonization, including Maria's mother, brothers, and sisters. Present, too, was Alessandro Serenelli.

In an era when the popular culture routinely trivializes sex and many adults believe teenagers are incapable of chastity, St. Maria Goretti receives little attention. At the same time, Maria has been the focus of charges that by canonizing her the Catholic Church proclaimed that "a woman is better dead than raped."[14]

On the contrary, perhaps the point of Maria Goretti's sainthood is that in the early-twentieth-century circumstances in which she lived, realizing "that her death was inevitable, she had every right to act as she did."[15] In a world where girls in many countries are subjected to violence and sexual victimization, perhaps—wrote Presbyterian author Kathleen Norris—it makes sense to have a St. Maria Goretti, who said, in effect, "Some things are worth dying for," who showed "some inner defiance, purity and strength that defies the sadist and the power of his weapons."[16] Indeed, "the mystery of hope, of holiness, infuses such defiance."[17]

In an addendum to the story of St. Maria Goretti, in March 1985 a sensational book was published by an Italian journalist, Giordano Bruno Guerri. The book called into question the entire saint-making process for the first and only time in modern history. The book, *Poor Assassin, Poor Saint: The True Story of Maria Goretti,* insisted that the church and the World War II Italian government of Benito Mussolini plotted together to fabricate the whole story. Because the book captured the attention of Italy's anti-Catholic press, the Vatican was forced to defend in public the integrity of its saint-making procedure.[18]

By attacking St. Maria Goretti, Giordano Bruno Guerri attacked a saint who had come to reflect the church's teachings on sexual virtue and responsibility. He declared that the evidence used against Alessandro Serenelli did not support his conviction, and he even implied that Maria had actually planned to let Alessandro have his way with her. Guerri also contended that Pius XII decided to make a saint out of Maria Goretti to counterbalance the sexual immorality of the American soldiers, most of whom were Protestants, who had liberated Italy in 1944.[19]

The Vatican responded by designating nine scholars from various fields to study Guerri's claims. Several months later, this commission issued a book that concluded that Guerri's book was nonsense. "He had, they argued, made hundreds of errors of fact as well as of interpretation. Guerri responded by threatening to sue the authors of the Vatican document for defamation."[20] In the end, however, Guerri could not prove the Vatican commission was wrong, so he abandoned his threat. In effect, the Guerri affair validated the Vatican's modern saint-making process.

As a parting note, in an era when the Catholic Church now officially opposes capital punishment, we might profitably ask ourselves, Would it have been better if Alessandro Serenelli had been executed for his crime? It took Serenelli more than two decades in prison to have a change of heart, but was this not preferable to killing him as an act of vengeful punishment?

St. John Vianney: Presbyter

One of the most beloved saints of modern times, **John Baptist Vianney (1786–1859)**, was born at Dardilly, France, near Lyons, at the peak of the French Revolution and spent his boyhood as a shepherd on his father's farm. He received little formal education, but early in life he was attracted to the priesthood. Because there was so much cultural and social unrest, and anti-Catholicism was widespread, John made his first confession and first communion secretly. When he was eighteen, he began his studies for the priesthood under the direction of the parish priest at Ecully, Abbé Balley.

Unfortunately, when it came to academics, John Vianney was not the brightest bulb in the chandelier. Discouraged in particular by difficulties with Latin, he made a pilgrimage to the shrine of St. John Regis at La Louvsc. Typically, young men studying for the priesthood were exempt from military service, but through an administrative error John was drafted into the army in 1809. Some sources say that John was mysteriously left behind when his unit departed. Others say that John willingly became a deserter. Whatever the case, in 1810 Napoleon granted a general amnesty to all deserters, and in 1813 John began formal studies for the priesthood at the major seminary at Lyons.

Once again, John Vianney encountered great difficulty with his studies, but through the intervention of Abbé Balley the young man was finally approved to become a priest. John's superiors decided that his good heart more than compensated for his lack of formal learning, and he was ordained at Grenoble in 1815. During the first years of his priesthood, John Vianney served as curate, or assistant pastor, alongside his old mentor, Abbé Balley, in Ecully.

When the abbé died in 1817, John Vianney remained in Ecully for a brief time; then in 1818 he was appointed as curé of Ars, an obscure rural village where most of the people were indifferent to religion. (*Curé* is a French term used for pastors, meaning, in effect, "caretaker of souls.") There he remained for the rest of his life.

As the curé of Ars, John Vianney spent his days in fasting and prayer. He visited every family in his parish, taught catechism, and largely by his preaching brought the people back to the practice of their faith. It took John about eight years to restore a lively religion to the lives of his people and reestablish the Christian life as the basis for family life and the life of the community. In 1824 John Vianney helped to establish a free school for girls. Three years later this school became La Providence, a home for orphans and deserted children.

Due to his lack of formal education, John was often treated scornfully and passed over by his superiors for assignment to more desirable parishes. All the same, John Vianney became famous far beyond Ars, due to his reputation in the confessional. Thousands of people traveled from all over France to have the curé of Ars hear their confession. Especially later in life, he spent many hours each day in the confessional, from midnight to early evening, leaving the long line of penitents only for Mass and his meals. For thirty years, John experienced disturbing phenomena, which he attributed to the devil.

John was attracted to the life of the Carthusians, an order of solitary monks, and three times he left Ars intending to find a life of solitary prayer. But each time he returned to help the people who came to him for spiritual guidance in ever larger numbers. As he grew old, important and influential people began to change their mind about the curé of Ars, and he was offered many honors, all of which he refused.

"Worn out by work and austerities," wrote Rev. Clifford Stevens, "John Vianney died on August 4, 1859, at the age of seventy-three."[21] He was canonized a saint in 1925.

CHAPTER SEVEN

Patron Saints Galore

There are patron saints for just about anything. Traditionally, people pray to a particular saint, asking for his or her prayers relative to whatever he or she is patron of. Sometimes a saint is patron of a particular situation, place, or cause due to an event in his or her earthly life. Other times, the connection is more or less accidental. "For example, St. Martin was the patron of 'drunkards' because his feast day, November 11, coincided with the Roman Vinalia, or Feast of Bacchus."[1]

Most patron saints are designated the patron of something as the result of popular devotion and long-existing custom. Relatively few patron saints were officially named as such by the church.

Here is a partial list of patron saints. Note that some vocations or needs or situations have more than one patron saint, and some saints have more than one patronal concern.

For a more complete list and more information about a particular saint, consult any good dictionary or encyclopedia of saints.[2]

Abandoned children: Jerome Emiliani

Accountants: Matthew (apostle)

Actors: Genesius

Advertisers: Bernardino of Siena

Alcoholics: John of God, Monica

Altar servers: John Berchmans

Animals: Francis of Assisi

Architects: Barbara, Thomas (apostle)

Art: Catherine of Bologna

Artists: Luke

Astronauts: Joseph of Cupertino

Astronomers: Dominic

Athletes: Sebastian

Authors: Francis de Sales

Automobile mechanics: Eligius

Aviators: Our Lady of Loreto, Joseph of Cupertino, Thérèse of Lisieux

Bakers: Elizabeth of Hungary, Nicholas of Myra

Bankers: Matthew (apostle)

Barbers: Cosmas and Damian, Louis IX (of France)

Blood banks: Januarius

Bodily ills: Our Lady of Lourdes

Booksellers: John of God

Boys: Nicholas of Myra

Brewers: Boniface, Augustine of Hippo, Nicholas of Myra

Bricklayers: Stephen

Brides: Nicholas of Myra

Broadcasters: Gabriel (archangel)

Builders: Vincent Ferrer

Bus drivers: Christopher

Butchers: Anthony the Abbot, Luke

Cabdrivers: Fiacre

Cancer patients: Peregrine Laziosi

Carpenters: Joseph

Catechists: Viator, Charles Borromeo, Robert Bellarmine

Charitable societies: Vincent de Paul

Chastity: Thomas Aquinas

Childbirth: Raymond Nonnatus, Gerard Majella, Margaret of Antioch

Children: Nicholas of Myra

Circus people: Julian the Hospitaller

Colleges: Thomas Aquinas

Comedians: Vitus

Communications personnel: Bernardino of Siena

Converts: Helena, Vladimir

Cooks: Lawrence, Martha

Dancers: Vitus

Dentists: Apollonia

Desperate situations: Jude (apostle), Gregory Thaumaturgus, Rita of Cascia

Disabled: Giles

Divorce: Helena

Dogs: Hubert

Drug addiction: Maximilian Kolbe

Dying: Joseph

Earache sufferers: Polycarp

Earthquakes: Emygdius

Ecologists: Francis of Assisi

Editors: John Bosco

Emergencies: Expeditus

Emigrants: Francis Xavier

Engaged couples: Agnes

Engineers: Ferdinand III

Expectant mothers: Raymond Nonnatus, Gerard Majella

Family: Joseph

Farmers: George, Isidore the Farmer

Fathers: Joseph

Firefighters: Florian

Flight attendants: Bona of Pisa

Florists: Thérèse of Lisieux

Forest workers: John Gualbert

Friendship: John the Divine

Funeral directors: Joseph of Arimathea, Dismas

Gardeners: Adalhard, Trypho, Fiacre, Phocas the Gardener

Good weather: Agricola of Avignon

Grandmothers: Anne

Grocers: Michael (archangel)

Grooms: Louis IX (of France)

Hairstylists (men): Martin de Porres

Hairstylists (women): Mary Magdalene

Hangovers: Bibiana

Headache sufferers: Teresa of Ávila

Heart-attack sufferers: Teresa of Ávila

Heart patients: John of God

Hemorrhoids: Fiacre

Homeless: Benedict Joseph Labre, Margaret of Cortona

Hotel employees: Julian the Hospitaller

Impotence: Winwaloe, Gummarus

Infants: Whyte, Nicholas of Tolentino

Infertility: Rita of Cascia

Janitors: Theobald Rogeri

Journalists: Francis de Sales

Lawyers: Ivo Hélory, Genesius, Thomas More

Librarians: Jerome

Medical technicians: Albert the Great

Mentally ill: Dymphna

Military: Theodore Tiro

Miscarriages: Dorothy, Bridget of Sweden

Mothers: Mary (mother of Jesus), Monica

Motorcyclists: Our Lady of Grace

Motorists: Christopher, Frances of Rome

Musicians: Cecilia, Dunstan, Gregory the Great

Nurses: Elizabeth of Hungary, Catherine of Siena

Pencil makers: Thomas Aquinas

Pharmacists: Cosmas and Damian, James the Great

Physical abuse: Pharaildis, Louise de Marillac, Fabiola

Physicians: Pantaleon, Cosmas and Damian, Luke,
    Raphael (archangel)

Pilots: Joseph of Cupertino

Plumbers: Vincent Ferrer

Police officers: Michael (archangel)

Postal workers: Gabriel (archangel)

Procrastination: Expeditus

Psychics: Agabus

Public education: Martin de Porres

Public relations: Bernardino of Siena

Race relations: Martin de Porres

Rain: Agricola of Avignon, Swithun

Rape victims: Agatha, Maria Goretti

Reconciliation: Theodore of Tarsus

Rheumatism: James the Great

Runaways: Alodia, Dymphna

Searchers of lost articles: Anthony of Padua

Seasickness: Elmo

Second marriages: Adelaide

Secretaries: Genesius

Security guards: Matthew (apostle)

Separation from a spouse: Gummarus, Nicholas von Flüe, Genulf

Singers: Gregory the Great, Cecilia

Single mothers: Margaret of Cortona

Skaters: Lidwina, Bernard of Montjoux (or Menthon)

Skiers: Bernard of Montjoux (or Menthon)

Sleep disorders: Seven Sleepers of Ephesus

Sleepwalkers: Dymphna

Social justice: Joseph

Social workers: Louise de Marillac

Songwriters: Caedmon

Stepparents: Adelaide

Sterility: Henry the Emperor

Stomachaches: Wolfgang

Stress: Walter of Pontoise

Students: Thomas Aquinas

Successful enterprises: Servatius

Swimmers: Adjutor

Teachers: Gregory the Great, Jean-Baptiste de La Salle

Teenagers: Aloysius Gonzaga

Telephone workers: Clare of Assisi

Television: Clare of Assisi

Therapists: Christina Ciccarelli

Throat ailments: Blaise

Toddlers: Vaast

Toy makers: Claude

Travelers: Anthony of Padua, Nicholas of Myra, Christopher, Raphael (archangel)

Truck drivers: Christopher

Veterinarians: Blaise

Volcanic eruptions: Agatha

Waitpersons: Martha

Whales: Brendan the Voyager

Widowers: Edgar the Peaceful

Widows: Paula

Wine merchants: Amand

Women in labor: Anne

Workingmen: Joseph

Young boys: John Berchmans

Young girls: Agnes

Zoos: Francis of Assisi

CHAPTER EIGHT

Saintly Details

Saints have an impact on Catholic faith and culture that non-Catholics often find perplexing. Everyplace you turn, it seems, you find saintly details. Any calendar that includes Catholic liturgical information seems to scatter each month with feast days for saints, both well known and obscure. Why do Catholics preserve and venerate the relics of saints, build shrines for saints, and name churches after saints? Why do Catholics sometimes carry *holy cards,* cards with pictures of saints or Mary on them? Why do they sometimes wear on a little chain around the neck a medal bearing the image of a saint or the Blessed Virgin Mary?

Why do Catholic churches often have statues of saints located in prominent places? What about all those candles you sometimes see in front of statues, especially in older churches, often in blue or red glass holders? Why do people light these candles, then kneel to pray before the statue? Finally, if there is one thing that makes a Catholic stick out in a crowd, it's the rosary. What is "this thing with the beads," anyway?

In this chapter we will turn our attention to the saintly details, the little but noticeable ways that the saints have an impact on everyday Catholicism. As you will see, it all adds up to a warm and wonderful spirit that helps Catholics to live their Christian faith in all-embracing, courageous, and light-hearted ways.

Saints are women and men who, by the grace of God, excelled at living their faith in this world. So spiritually hale and hearty were they that we have no reason to doubt that they are with God in eternal delight. Not only that, but we have reason to believe that they are still involved in the affairs of this world through their prayers on our behalf. Recall that no one is canonized unless it is proven beyond a shadow of a doubt that miracles—usually miraculous cures—took place through his or her prayers on behalf of the persons who experienced the miracles.[1]

The Catholic doctrine of the communion of saints expresses the ancient Christian belief that we who still thrash about in time and space have the saints as our spiritual companions. We believe, therefore, that we are far from alone, adrift on a beautiful planet, spinning through space, an insignificant dot in the Milky Way. Rather, we share life with one another in ways that transcend time and space, and load all things human and historical with divine meaning.

Because we belong to a transcendent community of grace, we take advantage of every opportunity to remind ourselves that we have friends in high places. Literally. Most of the saintly details can be explained in this manner. Most of the saintly details are simply ways to remind us that we belong to a community that transcends history. They remind us of the reality of our invisible but real friends, the saints. They are tangible ways to help keep ourselves in touch with intangible realities.

With this umbrella concept in mind, let's examine some of these saintly details.

Feast Days

When a person is beatified—the step just before canonization—he or she is assigned a day on the calendar that is designated as the saint's feast day. This does not mean that on every saint's feast day Catholics have a twelve-course meal and a party that goes on for hours. In some instances and in some places—think of St. Patrick's Day in New York City, Boston, or countless smaller cities—celebrations definitely take place, but the reasons are more ethnic and cultural than religious.

In fact, *feast day* is a rather obscure term that many Catholics are clueless about. It refers to a category in the hierarchy of liturgical observances, of which there are three: solemnities, feasts, and memorials. A *solemnity* refers to Masses that celebrate "events, beliefs, and personages of greatest importance and universal significance in salvation history."[2] There are more than a dozen solemnities each year, including Easter, Christmas, and All Saints (November 1).

A *feast day,* the middle category, is simply a liturgy of "lesser significance."[3] All saints' days are feast days, as well as days such as the Feast of the Holy Family (the Sunday after Christmas) and the Feast of the Triumph of the Cross (September 14).

The least-significant category, *memorials,* refers to liturgical observances important "only to a local country, church, or religious community" and are usually called *optional memorials.*[4] Examples are the liturgical celebration for Our Lady of Mount Carmel (July 16) and that for the Dedication of St. Mary Major, a church in Rome (August 5).

Relics

Of all the Catholic saintly details, it should be a snap to understand why Catholics preserve and venerate—meaning "to regard with respect and reverence"—relics. Many people today do something similar with great enthusiasm, and sometimes they spend large amounts of money in the process. In the secular sphere, relics are called memorabilia. Many people collect memorabilia related to celebrities from the world of sports. Cards bearing the pictures of great athletes are a big business. Collectors hoard anything and everything associated with great players of the past and present, including clothing, sports equipment, and photographs, and all the better if any of these items is autographed by the player. We hear periodically of some item that sold for hundreds of thousands of dollars merely because of its role in the life of someone famous. A ball or jersey autographed by basketball great Michael Jordan will only increase in value with time. Following the death of baseball star Joe DiMaggio in 1999, the value of DiMaggio memorabilia increased. The same goes for anything associated with a sports celebrity whom people admire and whose career they celebrate.

Collectors place great value on memorabilia associated with celebrities from the world of show business, too. Think of celebrities from the past such as Marilyn Monroe, Humphrey Bogart, and James Dean. Ditto for celebrities associated with popular music. Nothing is more collectible than memorabilia from the most popular rock group of all time, the Beatles. A lock of the late Beatle John Lennon's hair would bring a tidy sum, you may be sure.

Some people collect rare books. An autographed first edition of author Stephen King's first novel, *Carrie,* can easily bring between three and five thousand dollars. Collectors treasure autographed first editions by many lesser-known writers as well.

Saints are more than mere celebrities, but the impulse and spirit behind relics are similar to the impulse and spirit behind celebrity memorabilia. People want to be close to people they admire, and both celebrity memorabilia and saints' relics serve this purpose. They allow ordinary mortals, as it were, to feel closer to people they admire and from whose lives and work they gather inspiration. A football jersey worn and autographed by Joe Montana, perhaps the greatest quarterback who ever played the game, and a book in which St. Teresa of Ávila signed her name serve a similar purpose. They allow those who admire them to feel closer to them.

Once a celebrity dies, people visit his or her burial site as a way, once again, to feel closer to someone they held in great affection, although they may never have met the celebrity in person. The same goes for the burial sites of saints. People visit the tomb of St. Anthony of Padua, in Italy, because they admire him and want to feel closer to him.

Of course, there are some big differences between a celebrity and a saint. When a celebrity dies, fans continue to respect and treasure his or her memory, but that's about all. Conventionally religious fans of the celebrity may pray for him or her, may even be sure that the celebrity is "with God" or "in heaven." But, again, that's about it. Saints are another matter entirely.

As we have already seen, Catholics believe saints to be not only great figures from the past but great figures of the present as well. We, the church, hold up saints for public veneration. We believe that by the grace of God saints live with God in eternal delight, but they also continue to be interested in us and in our lives, and they pray for us when we ask them to. Relics are nothing more than bits and pieces left behind by the saint. We cherish these reminders of the saint's earthly life and of his or her continued existence in eternal joy just over there, not so far from us.

Technically, there are three kinds of relics. A first edition copy of *Oliver Twist,* by Charles Dickens, is valuable. But if that same book was autographed by Dickens, its value doubles or triples. The same principle holds with regard to relics. A *first-class* relic is the actual body, or part of the body, of a saint. It may strike us as gruesome to venerate a body, body part, or fragment of a saint's body, such as a tiny bit of bone. But this is no more gruesome than a fan of, say, John Lennon or Marilyn Monroe treasuring a lock of the celebrity's hair.

Cultural differences do enter into the mix, of course. In some cases, for example, if you visit the shrine of a saint, you will find that those who were alive when the saint died chose to preserve a body part associated with a particular gift the saint was known for. St. Anthony of Padua was famous as a great preacher, and if you visit his shrine in Padua, Italy, you will find his tongue in a special *reliquary*, a container for relics. If you visit St. Joseph's Oratory, on Mount Royal in Montreal, you will find the heart of Blessed André Bessette, a Holy Cross brother who lived in the early decades of the twentieth century and was widely known for his ability to

151

cure afflicted people by his prayers—always insisting, of course, that it was God, not he, who caused miracles to happen.

Centuries ago, people had a high comfort level with this idea of cherishing the bodies or body parts of saints after they died. Today, we may chuckle when we learn that after the death of St. Teresa of Ávila in sixteenth-century Spain, her body was scattered all over the map by people wanting to have a part of this great saint and mystic who was beloved by countless thousands.

Theologically, a first-class relic receives particular attention because the human body, according to St. Paul, is a "temple of the Holy Spirit" (1 Corinthians 6:19). In the case of a saint, this truth carries special meaning because he or she is known for great holiness—for being more alive and more loving than your average person.

Second-class relics are any articles or items used by the saint. This includes clothing, books, or anything the saint actually handled. If Mark McGwire ever becomes a saint (not likely, it's true), anything he wore, any bat he used, any ball he held or baseball glove he wore would be a second-class relic. A prayer book used by St. Teresa of Ávila is a second-class relic; so is the tattered habit worn by St. Francis of Assisi. The famous Shroud of Turin—if it is authentic, which it may or may not be—is a second-class relic, too, even though we're talking about the body of Jesus that may have touched the shroud, not that of a saint. The idea of a second-class relic isn't so unreasonable if you think of the fan who gets a thrill from holding the *very same guitar* a famous rock musician played. Or think of the collector who gets to hold a book Ernest Hemmingway actually held.

Really stretching things, a *third-class* relic is anything—*anything*—touched to a first-class relic. We might call this relic-by-association. If someone touches a rosary, for example, to the finger bone of St. Teresa of Ávila preserved in a church in Spain, that makes the rosary a third-class relic.

Relics are nothing more than sacred memorabilia. And the bottom line on relics, as it is on saints in general, is that Catholics can take them or leave them. Relics don't grab you? Fine. All the church asks is that you respect other people's feelings. If relics are helpful to your faith, all well and good. If they don't do a thing for you, this is not a problem. People who like relics shouldn't take them too seriously. People who don't get into relics should try to understand the legitimate theological basis on which the veneration of relics is founded.

"Respecting these material things has been more or less popular since the early Church," wrote Rev. Peter Klein, "varying according to era and culture. Mystique, exaggeration, and legend are common, and the Church is slow to offer official guarantees of authenticity; when it is established, she offers warm approbation."[5]

Shrines and Churches Named for Saints

In the United States alone, there are more than 150 shrines dedicated to Christ, Mary the mother of Jesus, and various saints.[6] According to the church's official Code of Canon Law, "The term *shrine* means a church or other sacred place which, with the approval of the local Ordinary [that is, bishop], is by reason of special devotion frequented by the faithful as pilgrims."[7]

In other words, a *shrine* is not an ordinary parish church, where a local faith community gathers for the liturgy. Rather, a shrine is a place set aside and dedicated as a place of pilgrimage, a place where travelers stop for prayer or devotional purposes. The custom of naming shrines, as well as parish churches, for a saint or for Mary under one of her many titles, goes back to the earliest Christian community. From the early days, it became traditional to celebrate the Eucharist at the place where martyrs were buried.[8] This was a way to honor the saint buried there and to include the saint in the prayers of the community.

By the third century, this practice had become universal. St. Augustine of Hippo remarked, "It is not to any of the martyrs, but to the God of the martyrs, although in memory of the martyrs, that we raise our altars."[9]

From this early practice developed the tradition of naming shrines and churches in honor of the saints, and the custom remains to the present day. A shrine is usually dedicated as a place of special devotion to a particular saint or to the mother of Jesus under one of her special titles (such as Our Lady of Guadalupe, Our Mother of Perpetual Help, Our Lady of Fatima). A shrine has a special focus on the saint it is named for, in a way that a parish church does not. People visit a shrine with the specific intention of praying to the saint to whom the shrine is dedicated. For example, the Shrine of St. Maximilian Kolbe in Libertyville, Illinois, attracts people who have a special devotion to a twentieth-century saint who gave his life for another man in Auschwitz, the World War II Nazi death camp.

Holy Cards, Holy Medals, and Statues

In any Catholic religious-goods store you will find an extensive display of religious medals, small medallions on which you will see an image of Mary or various saints. Two of the most popular subjects for such medals are St. Christopher and Mary under the title "the Immaculate Conception." St. Christopher is the patron saint of travelers, and both key rings and medals for display in cars are popular, even among many non-Catholics.

Immaculate Conception medals are something else. The story of this medal goes back to 1830 in Paris, France. Mary appeared to Catherine, a young novice in a convent.

The Lady stood, suspended in the air, to the right of the altar. She wore a robe as bright as the glow of dawn and a long veil that flowed to her feet. Her hair was in braids held by a bit of lace. "Her face," said Catherine, "was so beautiful that I cannot describe it."

The Lady stood upon a large white sphere, her feet resting on a greenish serpent. She stretched her hands toward the globe. Precious stones ornamented her fingers; from some of them, rays of light streamed toward the Earth, but the rest of the stones stayed dark. Just as Catherine was noticing this, the Lady said, "the rays of light are the graces that I shower on those who ask for them. . . . But there are graces for which I am not asked, and it is for this reason that the stones you see are not sending forth any rays of light."

Then an oval formed around the Lady, and around it Catherine saw the words, "O Mary, Conceived Without Sin, Pray for Us Who Have Recourse to Thee." The Lady said, "Have a medal made after this pattern. Those who wear it, blessed, around their necks, and who confidently say this prayer, will receive great graces and will enjoy the special protection of the Mother of God."[10]

Mary then showed Catherine the reverse side of the medal, on which was a monogram with the hearts of Jesus and Mary. Mary told Catherine to have medals struck with these images on them, to urge people to wear them, and to tell people that they would receive wonderful blessings if they cultivated a devotion to her through the use of this medal and its one-line prayer.

Before long, Catherine's story got out, and ever since, the Immaculate Conception medal has been one of the most popular, rivaled only by St. Christopher medals. Some Catholics wear the medal, many do not, and some wear it sometimes but not every day. As with all such things, it's entirely up to the individual, and nothing crucial hinges on the choice made. Some people find medals helpful to their spirituality; others do not. A medal can be a little reminder of the faith values you cherish or of a special devotion that is important to you. It's as simple as that.

The purpose of holy cards is similar. A baseball fan may put a favorite player's card on a bulletin board or refrigerator door or may carry the card in purse or wallet. Someone with a devotion to St. Jude or the Blessed Mother may put a holy card on a bulletin board or refrigerator door or may carry a card in purse or wallet. Some use holy cards as bookmarks. A holy card is merely a reminder of one's devotion to the saint whose image appears on the card. Many holy cards bear rosy, romanticized—sometimes even sappy—images, but we might as well have a sense of humor about it.

Finally, there is the matter of statues. There are still sectarian Christian groups that accuse Catholics of idol worship.

Nothing could be further from the truth. Ask even the simplest, most uneducated Catholic if Catholics worship statues, and you will get nothing but laughter in response. In Catholic churches you will often find statues of Jesus, Mary, Joseph, and other saints. Often a church will set up in an appropriate place a statue of the saint for whom the parish is named—St. Francis of Assisi, for example, or Mary, Queen of Heaven. The purpose of a statue is to remind us of the saint and help us relate to him or her.

Catholics often have statues of Jesus and various saints in their churches, and sometimes in their homes, for the same reason people display photographs of loved ones. They do it to remind themselves of heavenly persons who are special to them. If a Catholic "prays to" a statue, this happens only in the same way someone might "talk to" a photograph of a deceased loved one. You don't pray to the statue; you pray to the one the statue represents. The statue simply helps you to focus.

Vigil Candles

Often in Catholic churches, especially older ones, you see set up before statues of Mary and Jesus row upon row of stubby little candles in blue, red, amber, or clear glass cups, many of them lighted. Often there are also bigger candles that burn for a longer time. You don't need to hang around a

Catholic church for long before you see someone approach the statue and its attendant candles, drop some coins with a clatter into the slot of a nearby metal box, light one or more candles, then kneel to pray. Anyone unfamiliar with Catholic devotional practices may be mystified by such behavior. What in the holy heck is going on here?

Like most Catholic devotional customs, this one is fairly simple. Candles have a long history as symbols of prayer. There are lighted candles on the altar during every celebration of the Eucharist. The most symbolically laden candle is the huge Paschal candle—a sign of Christ, the light of the world—that is lit as part of the Easter Vigil liturgy each year, then relit for each Mass throughout the fifty days of the Easter season. On Pentecost, the Paschal candle is moved near the baptismal font or pool and lit only on the occasion of baptisms and funerals, as a sign of the Resurrection.

If you are observant, you will see candles used in many other ways as well. Sometimes a Catholic lights vigil candles, most commonly in front of statues of Jesus and Mary, as a continuing sign of the person's "prayerful vigilance of expectant faith." The person makes a monetary donation to cover the cost of the candle(s) and perhaps as a gift for charity. He or she then lights one or more candles, then pauses for a few moments of prayer. The candle remains lit until it burns out, a sign of ongoing prayer even after the person goes on with the day's activities.

The Rosary

The devotional prayer known as the Rosary has a history that goes back many centuries. Generically speaking, it even has a history that predates Christianity, but we won't go into that here.[11] The main thing to understand about the Rosary is that it is a repetitive form of prayer that has much to recommend it. The Rosary is a simple, Christ-centered, Marian devotional prayer that fits well with the human need to pray even when we find it difficult to put our feelings into words.

When you pray the Rosary, you typically use a rosary, a circular string of beads with an attached shorter string of beads that has a small crucifix or cross at its end. In the circle, there are fifty beads in five groups of ten, with a single, different bead between each set of ten.

You begin praying the rosary by making the sign of the cross, often using the little crucifix to do this. Then you recite the Apostles' Creed, the Our Father, three Hail Marys, and one doxology ("Glory be to the Father, and to the Son, and to the Holy Spirit . . ."). You keep track of the prayers by using the beads on the short strand attached to the circle of beads.

The purpose of all the beads is simply to keep track of how many prayers you have said. The beads give you something to hang on to. Psychologically, many people find this helpful. There is something about being able to hang on to those beads while praying that helps you maintain your attention and focus. In times of fear or anxiety, even at ordinary times, the beads give your hands something to do while you pray.

After the introductory prayers, you move to the circular part of the rosary and begin with the first bead. Each set of ten beads is dedicated to a *mystery*, and there are three sets containing five mysteries each: joyful mysteries, sorrowful mysteries, and glorious mysteries.[12] Most people who pray the Rosary have the mysteries memorized. All but two of these fifteen mysteries are taken directly from the Gospels and have to do with significant events in Jesus' life, which is why we can say that the Rosary is a Christ-centered devotional prayer. Traditionally, the joyful mysteries are used on Mondays and Thursdays, the sorrowful mysteries on Tuesdays and Fridays, and the glorious mysteries on Sundays, Wednesdays, and Saturdays. You meditate on only one of the three sets of five mysteries.

The repetitive nature of the Rosary, saying the Hail Mary over and over, is not based on the idea that the more prayers you say the better. Rather, the Hail Marys function something like a mantra does in Hinduism. There is nothing magical about the prayer; it's merely a way to occupy yourself on a conscious level while communing with God on a deeper level.

Theoretically, the purpose of the mysteries is to give you something to meditate upon while praying the Hail Marys, and this technique may work for some. Many, however, find that by the time you finish one set of ten Hail Marys your attention has wandered, and arriving at the bead for the next mystery jogs your mind and brings you back on track, until your attention wanders again. Someone once said, however, that one of the great things about the Rosary is that even if your mind wanders, at least your fingers keep on praying.

If you are not Catholic, the Rosary may sound complicated, perhaps bordering on mumbo jumbo. In practice, however, the Rosary is quite simple, a devotional prayer loved by countless Catholics—and even a few Protestants—the world over.[13]

Afterword: The Saints Celebrate the Imperfect

The saints are human beings who now live in eternal joy with God and with all of God's people who have slipped through the ever-so-thin veil between this life and the next. They were imperfect human beings in this life, but they accepted their own limitations, offered them to God, and did the best they could with what they had. In this, they offer us an example that we can follow by accepting our own imperfections and foibles and doing the best we can.

But the saints stand as examples we can emulate in another sense. The saints were aware that the church—meaning all of us and all of our church institutions, from the local parish to the Vatican in Rome—is far from perfect. They accepted with humility that living in the church sometimes means living with unsatisfactory responses to unsatisfactory situations. They accepted their own imperfections and handicaps, and they accepted the church's imperfections and handicaps, too.

The saints sometimes grew angry with church leaders and church policies, but they did not abandon the church. They stayed because they *believed* in the church and they believed *in the church.* They did not give up on the church, and they did not demand that the church measure up to their expectations and their standards of perfection as a condition for their remaining in the church.

The saints stayed because they knew that alongside all the church's personal and institutional flaws and shortsightedness there is the Spirit of the risen Christ, especially in the sacraments, particularly in the Eucharist. The saints believed with all their hearts in the real presence of the risen Christ in the Eucharist and in Holy Communion, and they believed that this Presence is found in its fullness in the Catholic Church. For this they stayed, even when church institutions and church leaders seemed less than Christian. For this they stayed, and for this they sometimes willingly died.

Many saints also remained faithful to Catholicism because they, too, were inspired by the example of saints who had gone before them. "Those from whom I receive the greatest consolations and encouragement," said St. Teresa of Ávila, "are those whom I know to be dwelling in Paradise."[1] In other words, the saints stayed with the church because the church is where they found the saints.

For the saints it mattered a great deal that the Catholic Church is most directly linked, through history and practice, to Christ, to his apostles, and to his mother. In spite of the church's infidelities large and small down through the centuries, the saints stayed. In spite of ways in which they themselves were hurt, offended, or scandalized by church people or church institutions, the saints stayed. In spite of everything, they stayed. The saints would agree with one of the great Catholic converts of the twentieth century, G. K. Chesterton: "I could not abandon the faith, without falling back on something more shallow than the faith. I could not cease to be a Catholic except by becoming something more narrow than a Catholic."[2]

We live in a time of instability in the church and in the world. In such a time, when we grow dissatisfied with conditions in the church—local, international, or both—or when we find ourselves personally hurt, offended, or scandalized by the church, we face the powerful temptation to walk away from the church, to choose another church or another religion as "just as good" or even "better." No one can see into the secret of another's heart, and no one should dare to judge another's conscience when it comes to such choices. All the same, the example of the saints can and should give courage and inspiration to stay when the temptation may be strong to leave. With the saints as our companions, we can refuse to settle for less.

Calendar of Saints

(does not include all saints)

January
1—Mary, Mother of God
4—Elizabeth Ann Seton
6—André Bessette
17—Anthony of Egypt
21—Agnes
29—Francis de Sales
31—John Bosco

February
1—Brigid of Ireland
3—Blaise
10—Scholastica

March
7—Thomas Aquinas
17—Patrick
19—Joseph
24—Gabriel (archangel)

April
16—Benedict Joseph Labre
23—George
26—Robert Bellarmine
29—Catherine of Siena

May
16—Brendan the Voyager
22—Rita of Cascia

June
2—Charles Lwanga
3—Kevin
13—Anthony of Padua
21—Aloysius Gonzaga
22—Thomas More
29—Paul (apostle)

July

6—Maria Goretti
19—Vincent de Paul
20—Margaret of Antioch,
    Wilgefortis
22—Mary Magdalene
24—Christina of Tyre
25—Christopher
26—Anne
27—Seven Sleepers of Ephesus
31—Ignatius of Loyola

August

4—Dominic,
   John Vianney
9—Edith Stein
10—Lawrence
11—Clare of Assisi
14—Maximilian Kolbe
20—Bernard of Clairvaux
27—Monica
28—Augustine of Hippo

September

9—Peter Claver
17—Hildegard of Bingen
30—Jerome

October

1—Thérèse of Lisieux
4—Francis of Assisi
8—Bridget of Sweden
15—Teresa of Ávila
18—Luke
28—Jude (apostle)

November

4—Charles Borromeo
5—Martin de Porres
13—Frances Xavier Cabrini
15—Albert the Great
18—Rose Philippine Duchesne
19—Elizabeth of Hungary

December

3—Francis Xavier
4—Barbara
21—Thomas (apostle)
26—Stephen
29—Thomas Becket

Notes

CHAPTER ONE: WHO ARE THE SAINTS?

1. One example of this tendency may be found in an otherwise excellent book: *Enduring Grace: Living Portraits of Seven Women Mystics*, by Carol Lee Flinders (San Francisco: HarperSanFrancisco, 1993). It is not what this book says that leaves the reader unsatisfied so much as what it does not say due to the author's academic, "outsider" status as she examines the lives and writings of Catholic saints and mystics. Because the author is not a Catholic, or even a Christian, and does not read the works of her subjects from within an ongoing subjective experience of the living Christian faith and tradition, her grasp of what her subjects said and what they stood for remains to a certain extent merely academic and therefore unbalanced and incomplete.

2. Kenneth L. Woodward, *Making Saints: How the Catholic Church Determines Who Becomes a Saint, Who Doesn't, and Why* (New York: Simon & Schuster, 1990), 64.

3. Matthew Bunson et al., *Our Sunday Visitor's Encyclopedia of Saints* (Huntington, Ind.: Our Sunday Visitor Publishing Division, 1998), 16.

4. See Peter Brown, *The Cult of the Saints: Its Rise and Function in Latin Christianity* (Chicago: University of Chicago Press, 1981), 50.

5. Augustine, *Against Faustus,* bk. 20. See Charles Dollen, *The Book of Catholic Wisdom* (Huntington, Ind.: Our Sunday Visitor Publishing Division, 1986), 40.

6. Bunson et al., 16.

7. Ibid.

8. Thomas Bokenkotter, *A Concise History of the Catholic Church,* rev. and exp. ed. (New York: Doubleday, Image Books, 1990), 60.

9. Quoted in Boniface Hanley, *Ten Christians* (Notre Dame, Ind.: Ave Maria Press, 1979), 250.

10. John Deedy, *A Book of Catholic Anecdotes* (Allen, Tex.: Thomas More Publications, 1997), 13.

11. Paul Tillich, quoted in Tony Castle, comp., *The New Book of Christian Quotations* (New York: Crossroad Publishing, 1982), 213.

12. One of the best examples of this is St. Benedict Joseph Labre (1748–83). Unsuccessful in attempts to join three different monastic orders, he became an itinerant pilgrim throughout Europe. He became known as the Beggar of Rome for his extreme poverty—never bathing, always dressing in filthy clothing.

13. Woodward, 17.

14. Ibid., 50.

15. Ibid., 59.

16. Ibid., 65.

17. Richard P. McBrien, ed., *The HarperCollins Encyclopedia of Catholicism* (San Francisco: HarperSanFrancisco, 1995), 219.

18. For these two anecdotes I am indebted to Woodward, 67.

19. Woodward, 66.

20. Bunson et al., 17.

21. McBrien, 219.

22. Woodward, 406.

1. Jacobus de Voragine, *The Golden Legend,* trans. William Granger Ryan, 2 vols. (Princeton, N.J.: Princeton University Press, 1993).

2. Herbert J. Thurston and Donald Attwater, eds., *Butler's Lives of the Saints,* 4 vols. (Westminster, Md.: Christian Classics, 1981).

3. John J. Delaney, *Dictionary of Saints* (New York: Doubleday, 1980). For shorthand purposes, I refer to those whom the church calls "blessed" — those who are not yet canonized and may never be—by the plural Latin *beati,* "blesseds."

4. Matthew Bunson et al., *Our Sunday Visitor's Encyclopedia of Saints* (Huntington, Ind.: Our Sunday Visitor Publishing Division, 1998).

5. Delaney, 9.

6. Christian Feldman, *God's Gentle Rebels* (New York: Crossroad Publishing, 1995), 4.

7. Ibid.

8. Ibid., 5.

9. Ibid., 7.

10. Ibid., 7–8.

11. *The Little Flowers of St. Francis,* trans. E. M. Blaiklock and A. C. Keyes (Ann Arbor, Mich.: Servant Books, 1985).

12. Omer Englebert, *St. Francis of Assisi: A Biography* (Ann Arbor, Mich.: Servant Books, 1979), 251.

13. Ibid., 268.

14. Ibid., 273.

15. Bunson et al., 260.

16. Thurston and Attwater, 4:12.

17. Ibid., 4:13.

18. Ibid.

19. Ibid.

20. Ibid.

21. St. Thérèse of Lisieux, *Story of a Soul,* trans. John Clarke (Washington, D.C.: ICS Publications, 1976).

22. Thurston and Attwater, 4:13.

23. Ibid., 4:14.

24. St. Thérèse of Lisieux, 199.

25. The translation of these Scripture verses is that given by John Clarke in the introduction to his translation of *Story of a Soul* (p. viii).

26. St. Thérèse of Lisieux, 221.

27. Thurston and Attwater, 4:14.

28. Ibid., 4:15.

29. Ibid.

30. Monica Furlong, *Thérèse of Lisieux* (New York: Pantheon Books, 1989), 120.

31. Ibid., 128.

32. Thurston and Attwater, 3:52.

33. Ibid., 3:53.

34. Ibid.

35. Ibid.

36. Ibid., 3:54.

37. Ibid. The scriptural reference is to the Acts of the Apostles 7:57–60.

38. Feldman, 187.

39. Ibid., 188.

40. Thurston and Attwater, 4:111.

41. Feldman, 154.

42. Thurston and Attwater, 4:111.

43. St. Teresa of Ávila, *The Autobiography,* trans. E. Allison Peers (New York: Doubleday, Image Books, 1962), 88.

44. Feldman, 159.

45. Delaney, 542.

46. Thurston and Attwater, 4:119.

47. Feldman, 182.

48. Ibid.

49. Ibid., 183.

50. Ibid., 185.

51. Thurston and Attwater, 4:120.

52. Ibid.

53. Feldman, 185.

54. Peter Klein, ed., *The Catholic Source Book* (Dubuque, Iowa: Brown Publishing–Roa Media, 1990), 362.

55. Thurston and Attwater, 3:426.

56. Ibid.

57. Ibid.

58. See Gerald O'Collins and Edward G. Farrugia, *A Concise Dictionary of Theology* (Mahwah, N.J.: Paulist Press, 1991), 133.

59. Feldman, 68.

60. Thurston and Attwater, 4:429.

61. Feldman, 79.

62. Thurston and Attwater, 4:430.

63. Ibid., 4:431.

64 Feldman, 84–85.

65. Ibid., 90.

66. Ibid.

67. Ibid.

68. Ibid., 93.

1. Jaroslav Pelikan, *Mary through the Centuries: Her Place in the History of Culture* (New Haven, Conn.: Yale University Press, 1996), 222.

2. Sally Cunneen, *In Search of Mary* (New York: Ballantine Books, 1996), 24.

3. Ibid., 5.

4. Adela Yarbro Collins, "The Apocalypse (Revelation)," in *The New Jerome Biblical Commentary* (Englewood Cliffs, N.J.: Prentice Hall, 1990), 1008.

5. Elizabeth A. Johnson, "Blessed Virgin Mary," in *The HarperCollins Encyclopedia of Catholicism,* ed. Richard P. McBrien (San Francisco: HarperSanFrancisco, 1995), 833.

6. Cunneen, 147.

7. Ibid. As quoted in Hilda Graef, *Mary* (Westminster, Md.: Christian Classics, 1985), 1:205.

8. Cunneen, 147.

9. Johnson, 834.

10. Charles Dickson, *A Protestant Pastor Looks at Mary* (Huntington, Ind.: Our Sunday Visitor Publishing Division, 1996), 40.

11. Cunneen, 208.

12. Ibid.

13. Ibid., 219–20.

14. Ibid., 220.

15. Ibid.

16. Ibid.

17. Ibid., 222.

18. Kathleen Coyle, *Mary in the Christian Tradition,* rev. N. Am. ed. (Mystic, Conn.: Twenty-Third Publications, 1996), 102.

CHAPTER FOUR: THOROUGHLY MODERN SAINTS

1. Quoted in Boniface Hanley, *Maximilian Kolbe: No Greater Love* (Notre Dame, Ind.: Ave Maria Press, 1982), 21.

2. Anne Gordon, *A Book of Saints: True Stories of How They Touch Our Lives* (New York: HarperCollins, 1994), 78.

3. Hanley, 23.

4. Ibid., 24.

5. Quoted in Gordon, 80.

6. Ibid.

7. Ibid., 81.

8. Ibid., 77.

9. Ibid., 131.

10. Ibid.

11. Ibid., 132.

12. Ibid.

13. Quoted in Robert Ellsberg, *All Saints* (New York: Crossroad Publishing, 1997), 344.

CHAPTER FIVE: LEGENDARY SAINTS AND LEGENDS ABOUT REAL SAINTS

1. Bunson et al., 164.

2. Ibid.

3. Thurston and Attwater, 3:297.

4. Ibid.

5. Ibid., 3:298.

6. Voragine, 1:38.

7. Thurston and Attwater, 3:195.

8. Ibid.

9. Ibid.

10. T. S. Eliot, *Murder in the Cathedral,* in *T.S. Eilot: The Complete Poems and Plays* (New York: Harcourt, Brace, 1962), 196.

11. Ibid., 199.

12. Ibid., 209.

13. Ibid., 213.

CHAPTER SIX: SAINTS OF MANY KINDS

1. Woodward, 55.

2. Ibid.

3. See, for example, David G. Myers, *The Pursuit of Happiness* (New York: Avon Books, 1992), 162: "Seven recent studies concur that, compared to couples who don't cohabit with their spouses-to-be, those who do have *higher* divorce rates."

4. Delaney, 237.

5. Quoted in Feldman, 32.

6. Ibid., 61.

7. Clifford Stevens, *The One Year Book of Saints* (Huntington, Ind: Our Sunday Visitor Publishing Division, 1989), 162.

8. Ibid.

9. Woodward, 123.

10. Other sources say that Maria was murdered in the kitchen. See, for example, Kathleen Norris, "Maria Goretti," in *Martyrs,* ed. Susan Bergman (Maryknoll, N.Y.: Orbis Books, 1996), 300.

11. Ibid., 306.

12. Ibid., 304.

13. Woodward, 123.

14. Eileen J. Stenzel, "Maria Goretti: Rape and the Politics of Sainthood," in *Violence Against Women,* ed. Elizabeth Schussler Fiorenza and M. Shawn Copeland, Concilium Series (Maryknoll, N.Y.: Orbis Books, 1994), quoted in Norris, 300.

15. Norris, 308.

16. Ibid.

17. Ibid.

18. Woodward, 122.

19. Ibid., 124.

20. Ibid.

21. Stevens, 224.

CHAPTER SEVEN: PATRON SAINTS GALORE

1. Klein, 367.

2. The author wishes to thank the authors and editors of the following reference sources, from which this list is compiled: Matthew Bunson et al., *Our Sunday Visitor's Encyclopedia of Saints* (Huntington, Ind.: Our Sunday Visitor Publishing Division, 1998); John J. Delaney, *Dictionary of Saints* (New York: Doubleday, 1980); and Peter Klein, ed., *The Catholic Source Book* (Dubuque, Iowa: Brown Publishing–ROA Media, 1990); *Our Sunday Visitor's Catholic Almanac* (Huntington, Ind.: Our Sunday Visitor Publishing Division, 1999).

CHAPTER EIGHT: SAINTLY DETAILS

1. See Bunson et al., 17: "Miracles are required for each step of the process, from venerable status to canonization, and these miracles must be authenticated by competent sources, such as medical practitioners and competent consultations."

2. Klein, 302.

3. Ibid.

4. Ibid.

5. Ibid., 381.

6. See *Catholic Shrines and Places of Pilgrimage in the United States* (Washington, D.C.: United States Catholic Conference, 1992).

7. *The Code of Canon Law in English Translation* (Grand Rapids, Mich.: William B. Eerdmans, 1983), can. 1230.

8. This practice may be what lies behind words in the book of Revelation: "When he opened the fifth seal, I saw under the altar the souls of those who had been slaughtered for the word of God and for the testimony they had given" (6:9).

9. Quoted in Kevin Orlin Johnson, *Expressions of the Catholic Faith* (New York: Ballantine Books, 1994), 204.

10. Ibid., 242.

11. For a brief history of the Rosary, see Richard McBrien, ed., *The HarperCollins Encyclopedia of Catholicism* (San Francisco: HarperSanFrancisco, 1995), 1137. For a detailed discussion of the Rosary and its history, see Richard Gribble, *The History and Devotion of the Rosary* (Huntington, Ind.: Our Sunday Visitor Books Publishing Division, 1992).

12. For a list of all the mysteries, consult any basic book on Catholicism, such as *The Essential Catholic Handbook* (Liguori, Mo.: Liguori Publications, 1997), 69; or John O'Holohan, comp., *Pocket Prayer Book* (Ann Arbor, Mich.: Servant Publications, 1988), 50. For an in-depth look at all the mysteries, see David Burton Bryan, *A Western Way of Meditation: The Rosary Revisited* (Chicago: Loyola Press, 1991), 109–41.

13. See Dickson, especially chapter 17, "The Rosary Is for Everyone."

AFTERWORD: THE SAINTS CELEBRATE THE IMPERFECT

1. Quoted in Jill Haak Adels, *The Wisdom of the Saints* (New York: Oxford University Press, 1987), 5.

2. G. K. Chesterton, *The Well and the Shallows* (London, 1935), 71–72.

Index of Saints